MOODS OF
WAR

By

James Love

A Soldier & A Poet

There are some that write about war and sometimes they try and glorify it.
I think that if you write about war, you must have to have been in one.
For truly there is no glory.
Only adrenaline, sadness, and sometimes regret.
Not forgetting the dead.
In wars one must never forget the dead.
For the dead are the reason we are living.
All Hail the Dead.
All Hail My Brothers.
Long Live the Dead.

ACKNOWLEDGEMENTS

With regard to my time served in the military. I would say wholeheartedly it has been enlightening to me. In regard to the concept of fear, irrationality, and the Regimental system. of the tenacity of the British Airborne Soldier, of all of those who have to pass a selection process. In order to join Regiments and units from within the elitist Regiments of the British Forces and others throughout the world. In reality and the world as I've seen it.

Everybody fucked up somewhere, somehow. Some paid for it with their lives whether as a direct consequence of the individual actions or lack of, or of mistakes or failings by others.

There are those who know of these things from 82, and behind closed doors late into the night and into the early hours, these incidents may sometimes surface through alcohol and maudlin minds.

But only in class.

Never Forgotten, the Class of 82.

Jim Love, 2021

Fifteen men of 'em stiff and stark
Yo ho ho and a bottle of rum
Ten of the crew had the murder mark
Yo ho ho and a bottle of rum

R L Stevenson

The inky blackness of the night's sky was slowly giving way to the deep blue of the dawn. The stars, spluttering like candles. Giving one last flicker, then once again, lost in the depths of space. Behind him, the moon. Like some silvery white disc, suspended on invisible wires, giving shape and shadow, but no definitive colour. The water. Still, unmoving. Its surface akin to a giant mirror, reflecting images, so out of place, so foreign, that, had it not been for the cold crisp air that bit with each breath. If he blinked, it would surely vanish before him. Numbed, not only with cold, but with what was about to take place. He stood like the others, bent slightly forward. Head bowed, like some pagan ceremony, designed to appease the gods. However, it was not the burden of responsibility, that caused this seemingly mass display of humbleness. It was the massive weight of their Bergens, weapons, ammo. For this was the 21st of May 1982, 0200hrs Zulu. Their destination: "BLUE BEACH TWO".

Gnr JM Love
2 Para Group A Coy 2Para
Foo Party Signaller
29Bty 4th FD Regt RA (Para Contingent).

I've not much understood life, nor love.
I hope comprehending death, is easier.

Bend and kiss me now,
For it may be the last before our death.
And when that's over, we'll be different,
Imperishable things, a cloud or a fire.
And I know nothing but this body, nothing
But that old vehement, bewildering kiss.

Keats

CONTENTS

1) Death's Smokey

Death's Smokey
Cloud...
Smoke filled my eyes,
Burned my lungs...
Took away the colours,
Turned it all to grey.
It moved within the wind.
Leaving behind,
Blackened remains.
It clung to my clothes
Like a cape, made in hell.
It's an image, I try to forget.
But it's hard.
For, whenever I see, grey smoke.
I remember...
That
Smell

2) May 82

It rained,
And I heard it fall.
Maybe not every drop...
But almost all.
We cut the turf,
And stacked it high.
Two foot thick,
And just as wide.
Rain ran down my face,
While it filled the hole.
Soaked my clothes,
Washed my soul.
No gentle pitter-patter this,
It crashed.
The wind howled and blew,
As the bayonets slashed.
All the while,
Eight thousand miles away.
You cheered...
Got drunk,
And slept

In a cosy warm bed.

3) Bullets Marked

Some buzzed...
While others, whizzed.
I felt their breath...
And I, shrank smaller.
Though, lots passed...
and I never,
... heard a sound.
But I saw, where they went.
I saw,

Who... they found.

4) A Battle's Roar

Simply, music...
To my ears.
So, sing your songs, and...
Beat your drums.
To the staccato, rock 'n' roll...
My lungs are full cordite,
While my head's filled, with,
The whispering sound.
Of the, gimpy's... roar!
It's in sync, with the crump, 'n' thump,
Of the falling, of... the shot.
Of dirt, and dust, and sandy graves.
Rewards... just bits of tin...

A symphony of sound.
A lousy lullaby...
To help you sleep.
When...
Faraway

In Foreign lands...

5) *Play it Again Sam, For I'm*

Stirring stuff, they played...
as we march along.
We are singing... dead men's songs...
Melodies... centuries old.
Of flesh and bones,
that create bonds.
Where we empathise with,
Deeds of glory...
Of which are merely,
Heroic tales that only tell half our story.
Lullabies or crooning
Crude, raucous or dreaming.
We are writing history...
my friends.
Blood-soaked minutes, every a one.
The booze burns... as it goes down.
And fists smash the table.
We sing, and drink, and chant!
For those dead, gone, and

Unable.

6) Fitzroy

Low and fast,
That's how they came.
Screaming low across the ground...
I swear.
If I'd tried.
I could have touched it, as it passed.
A trail of death and devastation,
They'd left behind.
Where the rising black plumes of smoke,
Lay testament to that.
The dead, the maimed,
Trapped on a floating inferno.
In that brief moment.
Fathers, sons and brothers, Died
The lucky ones that lived.
Bleeding, burnt and scarred, shocked.
Not now, the men I once knew.

Author's Notes/Comments:
I can always visualise the grinning Sky Hawk pilot as he
passed.

7) In Mud and Filth We Lay and...

To be proud of someone,
You need to know, what they've done!
As the horsemen of the apocalypse waited...
A warrior's heart, from another time... Lay dormant.
Trying, to make sense, of earthly, realities.
Like a dog...
That's caught, a scent... on the wind.
It sparked.
While they spoke in Sogdian.
They smiled, that macabre grin.
With a Fibonacci rose, upon...
their chests.
Skeletal mounts, pawed the ground,
biding... their time.
Their riders' grotesque laugh cut across the wind.
And sent a shiver, down the spine.
Of every man.
And still...
We

waited... For the dawn.

8) Like a Dantesque

Death's Call.
It screamed... like,
a Banshee's... wail...
Its breath...
It pushed... my chest, so hard.
It touched, my spine.
Time, stopped still... for a, moment.
While an eerie silence reigned.
Then, the ground erupted!
Fire and molten metal shards
Cut through the air.
Bringing further screams, from the maimed, and
dying.
Adding, voices to...
Hell's

Choir.

9) *A Call To War, a Call to*

There's a greyish-ness to the dawn.
When black, slips... to blue.
Where the obscure, lays, in between...
Where Death, hones... his scythe.
Where there is, a... stillness.
Where oft, soldiers pause,
and reflect.
There are no words...
Before the coming of the dawn.
Nor sounds, 'cept, of the dead man's, whistle!
The prelude...
To

Death

10) An Odyssey In

I had no taste,
For my mouth was dry.
My empty stomach...
Knotted from its pit.
I felt no fear...
Nor never felt, the cold!
The night was still...
But not for long.
Soon to be heard,
Was the pale horses' song.
And death swept down amidst,
The screaming shells...
Whilst Valkyries,
took their choice.
Brave men lived, and died,
While we let our bullets fly.
On those mountains,
During June.
In

1982.

11) As Symbolic Whistles Blew

Side by side, we lay.
Within an arm's distance.
Prelude, to a dawn...
Each man's thoughts... his own.
No sound, save the wind.
Which brought that battle's din.
All lost within... blue-grey black,
Death's favourite colour.
A mountain to climb
Just beyond the river.
Soon we'll see the sun.
Soon well get up run...
Soon it will be over.
Soon we'd...
Dance to

Death's soulful tune

12) We Called Out in the Rain

It cut, like a thousand knives.
It bit deep.
While invisible fingers tore and...
And tried to rip us, off our feet.
Skin... turned blue, then grey.
Like how the sky's, colour changed.
And love left our hearts...
True emotion replaced by
Duty... and devotion.
Only,

To one another.

13) The Gulf, The Ghan, the Middle East

I looked at the devastation.
The pictures of the maimed.
Headlines that screamed!
For the dead it portrayed.
But it's not my war I said!
Mine had fields of yellow, blue vistas.
We fought for Britain, and its crown.
But you'd not know that...
But I still hear the gunfire, the shellfire,
and the bombs.
Though I no longer stand amidst...
Those windswept, fields of gold.
A part of my heart, is always... there!
For that was my war...
And it was a bit further south.

14) May 26th 1982...

It shut out the sun, turning the sky black
It gathered impetuous pushing them over,
malevolently…
like a roaring express train, loosened from its tracks…
Careering wildly, across fields.
Its force… striking at exposed flesh.
Pummelling bodies, knocking them over like skittles.
Winter, had arrived…

On the fifth day it snowed.

15) Chronophobia, it Still and I See Them Row

I can't wait,
for the coming snows...
To cleanse my soul...
I trade, in times, of secrets...
Of the deeds, of the dead.
With only those, who knows.
When grey skies, turn black.
And winter's chills, call...
It's the devil, who's...
Trying to claim, your soul.
While the skies change, again.
Black to grey, and then, to bluish white.
Snowflakes swirl...
Like the screams, of the dying.
They envelop your body, and stick.
Drowning out reality.
Soaking lashes, blinding all who see.
Draining life.
I'll always remember.
Each time, it snows.
 Snow... cladding, corpses...
Lying there row

On row.

16) 7.62mm... It's Life's Chorus

I like, the oily cold feel of the metal.
The menacing, blue-black sheen.
As it slowly warms... in...
my hands.
It's a comforting weight...
It moulds... to my soul.
Like Judas, it holds twenty!
It's an international currency,
Pointed, copper coated...
... bits of lead
That crack and thump,
800 feet per second...
... as they, pass through the air.
That whizz 'n' splat... it takes...
Its pound of flesh.
As it tears its way, on its path.
Fist-size holes appear.
Delivering, its...
Message

Of Death.

17) Could I Say... To What

For...
I have seen the likes,
That, few, have ever seen...
I've inhaled,
the breath,
from
A dying man's... Last words.
I've been immersed, in the van of battle.
I've watched dispassionately.
While brothers died.
I shared death's banquet.
I've seen the sun... bloody red, whilst it set.
Never, expecting to see it, rise.
I have learned the truth, about... dying,
and the cost,
To men, at war.
I've tasted cordite, mingled with fear.
Death has no pact with destiny.
And I'm drinking with,
the lost,
the forgotten,
and the dead.
I've saved the world
And it's been inherited
By

The snowflakes, from hell.

18) Until

Until you have had the ground,
beneath your feet,
disappear.
Seen the sky, turn black,
and, shower you... with,
molten metal fragments.
You'll never know, how precious,
the morning can be,
for men, at war.
I pray you never have to
share the moment.

19) The Wind of War Roared

Not me...
And I screamed...
And I ran, faster.
Not me
And, I laughed...
While, on I zigged.
Then, I zagged.
The tears, streaked...
My cheeks.
And the air, was... filled
With, lead
My lungs burned.
As the smoke,
Blocked out the sun.
I was down.
Then...
I pushed myself up again.
And

I began to run...

20) What I've Shared, I've Shared

Earth, sand, and mud.
From holes, all over the world.
We'd stare, at the skies, and stars...
Share our secrets, trade our desires.
Thinking of home, wherever that was.
Thinking of those we loved...
Of those, we'd hope to meet.
Hoping not to die.
There was a calmness, amidst it all.
A silent longing...
An empathy, greater than any other.
For, I shared those holes

With my airborne brothers.

21) *Saddle Up the Horses of the Apocalypse*

My arcs aren't clear... yet.
All this I see before me...
It's... my life!...
I've done a three-metre check,
Death's got my six.
"P hour," may still remain... undecided.
But I've already crossed life's start line!
We'll be going in hot.
Though the enemy strength unclear.
It won't be clean fatigue.
From the DZ to the feba.
I'll continue to tab, till I hit that FRV.
What I do know...
I won't be alone!
Stand by, brothers... and get ready,
to open the gates of "Valhalla".

We're going home!

22) *You'll Never Know Nor Share*

I'm just sad.
Because I can't,
Share...
No words...
No thoughts...
You weren't there!
How can you say
You know... ?
Did you,
See his head explode?
Or feel the spray of blood
As it hit your face?
Never to forget
No semblance of a
Cloth
Only in darker-times
Can you...
Feel it all.

Like yesterday!

Extract from the diaries of "Jock Love A Soldier & A
Poet: In The Field of Battle: Times Were Harsh".

23).My Thoughts Stray, To...

Darkness.
Don't pray for me...
I'm past redemption...
My deeds, outweigh my faith.
I'll languish... in that great hall.
Drinking,
With my brothers.
Until that final battle.
Dead men, can't die.
My love now lies, immortal.
And lonely now I sit.
Waiting for that war.
They call

Ragnarök...

24) Frangere a Malady I

Need to know.
Doctor, doctor...
Can you tell me why...?
I'm drinking vodka,
trying to drown away, my sleep!
And why
There are no songs, that laud my friends.
Though the memories, still run deep.
And though you think, I'm listening to you...
Even while you speak.
I'm 8 thousand miles away...
On a southern, summer's day.
At bottom, of, the world...
I'm toasting warriors.
And the moment, makes me smile.
I see them all, just like, yesterday.
Then I see them as they fall.
When I'm alone at night.
Their silent screams invade my dreams.
Preventing me from sleep.
I saw Death in all his forms.
And though he passed me by,
I have a bond, with brothers,
That even death

Can't break.

25) Death, We Taste...

Come sweet death,
Bringer of the dawn.
Leave me tranquil...
While innocents, sleep.
Come sweet death,
Harvester, of light.
Show me the path,
Through, the darkest of night.
Come sweet death...
Your warm, embrace.
Turns to ice, at spider's touch.
While the dying, says it all.
Come sweet death...
Our mission of life,
Tainted, by the smell,
Of...

our own blood.

26) Adrenaline

Tracer lit the night
While the screams of the dying
Were drowned out
By the exploding shells.
No longer cold or wet
No thoughts of hunger.
Just a surge, a rush

The body'd come alive.

27) All That You Know

It's dark, but you know that.
It's cold and it's windy,
while the rain lashes down.
There's a feeling in the pit of your stomach.
It's dark, but you know that.
It's dark, but you know that.
You all rise together, in your extended line.
You squelch towards the summit.
Returning fire at the flashes in front.

It's dark, but you know that.

28) Arctic Socks...

My feet are cold.
How many of us feel that?
A paddle on the beach...
Whose chill, bit deep.
And thirty years on,
The pain prevents my sleep.
Who would have thought that?
Because of what, was once done.
My feet are cold,

Thirty years on...

29) First Light

It's dark, but not quite,
It's almost day, but not quite.
Half haze, grey gloom, but not quite.
Not red, not green, not black, not white:
Almost day, almost, but not quite.
When you differentiate between colours
You've got first light:

Almost day, almost, but not quite.

Author's Comments:
Company Sarn't Major Colin Price and I shared a cigarette,
on Goat Ridge. He explained first light to me.

30) I Left Him Waiting... For

Still...
Now calm, almost serene.
There was a lull,
In the noise.
He lay there: his...
Eyes still blue,
But opaque,
Going milky... grey.
Hand outstretched.
For help?
Or to...
Welcome

God?

31) Je Touché Moi

Death passed me by,
but he touched my soul.
While his scythe of fiery lead,
cut a swathe through the pre-morn light.
Bony fingers plucked holes in mortal flesh,
To quench the reaper's thirst.
He passed me by,

This time.

32) *In The Ghan, You Run With a*

Tightly in my arms I'd held him,
No chance to staunch the flow.
The face was changing colour:
Ruddy pink, a sickly puce,
Then indigo.
He tried to speak...
Now it's a chalky, bluish white.
A single tear it fell,
While I, tried not to weep.
But looking down, I saw...
That half his head... was gone!
"They're on their way,
Hang on in there," I heard me say.
But his eyes had lost focus,
Slowly dimmed, and the spark...
Just went out.
He'd bled where he fell...
His warrior's journey... over.
While mine... had just begun!
And every time, I close my eyes.
My journey... starts its run.
I relive that bloody moment.
In that dusty... Afghan sun.
Where I lost... my best mate:
A greater friend, and true.
Shot down dead...
By a,
Dirty... motley...

Crew.

33) I Have Gone, But There Are Those

No more figures of eight,
No klaxons call.
Of ships making waves:
Phosphoric shafe,
or their light trails...
of death.

With their ever-omnipresent images,
Those that sadly sank.
Have at last, finally settled...
Their final breath.
That silent trail of bubbles...
ended.

Meanwhile the birds
Have once again... reclaimed,
their skies!
Those metal predators,
which screamed along the sound:
Mere echoes... of the mind.

Where now the islands
and her shores
Are quiet... nay idyllic... once again,
Are as silent... as are those,
Who now lay...
'neath its soil and its sea

who still guard them.

34) My Friend Died...

"Look... flowers," he said.
And as he pointed
I saw where poppies grew.
"Weeds, just weeds..." said I,
And I bent back down...
To stem his blood's flow.
I tried... with words, of comfort,
To reassure my friend
But it was his mother...
...with whom he talked
In the end.
As weeds and flowers swayed
Death... took my friend
While God,
Looked on

On that day.

35) We Were Near the Hill

And through the smoke,
Amidst the battle's thrall,
I heard a comrade speak!
It warmed my heart,
and quelled, the fear,
that lay deep inside.
And it did make me laugh...
"Where the fucking hell have you been?" he said
As shells rained down and bullets flew.
"I got lost," I said,

... In the gully at Darwin in 82.

36) The Silent Few

We trained for war,
Lived violent lives.
Fresh-faced boys,
With pretty wives.

To keep the peace,
To end aggression.
Oust the foe,
Perhaps teach a lesson.

Of foreign shores,
Sand mud and shit.

But British soil,
For we now lie in it.

My name,
Unknown.
A mother's son,
So far from home.

37) The British

Truly
Brave men died here today.
Did the swaying grass bring forth your tears?
Will this land that touched,
Nay claimed your soul
Stay serene forever, and remain theirs now?
Or will man's greed once more
Bring forth the havoc that is war
To find our children
Or God forbid our children's children
So they too, will one day lay
Beneath that foreign soil
That we now call the

Empire!

38) Orders

We crouched:
We blended in.
Smoking cigarettes,
While we waited.
Waited to be told, what to do.
When,
and by who? Meanwhile
All around the chaos ensued
Men died
The battle dragged on
We waited
Death waited

For War

39) *Left A Bit And Left A Bit*

Left a bit
and left a bit
and left a little more.
Now add a bit
and add a little more.
The arc's not high, as you watch it fly.
Though the chattering rattle, amidst all the battle,
causes your ears to roar.
One belt down, fifty rounds, tracer one in four.
Now left a bit

and left a bit...

Author's Notes/Comments:
I got a hard time because I didn't have any link for the
machine guns.
But I had a set of laser binos. So, spotted for them.

40) Airborne Brothers

We have endured much
Though said little
Some have not survived
While all around the world
Peoples are now freer
As a consequence of
our deeds

41) In Sunny Glades From Barren Stone

Cold and sombre,
Quiet in their dreams.
Row on row... They stand.
Men etched on stone.
Forever is forever.
But here they stand...
...together.

And silence is their call.

42.) It's Darkest...

His breath...
turned to frost,
on the blades of grass...
Stars...
like pinpricks, in the heavens.
Seemed only inches
from his face.
His body merged with the planet,
And he made his peace with God.
Then he was up and moving...
Forward...
ever forward.
Fear and trepidation surged,
Into adrenalin.
And the night came alive...
With flashes of coloured light,
Bringing death...

Before the dawn.

43) *I Am I Said...*

I am a soldier...
It's what I do.
I know no other:
I am a soldier...
St Michael
Is my protector.
I am a soldier...
It's in my blood;
It's who I am.
I am a soldier...
The smell of Death,
Still lingers.
I am a soldier...
I'm known,
Unto God.

I am a warrior.

44) *It's Time I...*

With opaque eyes
He... watched me
As we shared
The moment
That lasted... for eternity.
I spoke his name...
I shook him roughly...
But the answer
Was just the same.
Behind my back...
Death smiled.
And

Moved on.

45) A Call To War As...

In the hall of the slain
in mighty Asgard
Called Valhalla,
Odin said to Eriksmal...
The Fólkvangr's had its fill!
Send forth the Valkyries for more Einherjar.
Before the sun sets on Glasir c
Or Eikþyrnir eats all Læraðr's leaves.
Find more like them...
From that place called Arnhem!
There've been fresh battles.
Scour the fields of Goose Green.
The slopes of Longdon,
Seek out their brothers!
Before...

Ragnarök begins.

46) Cows' Eyes... They Looked Like

His eyes bulged;
He looked down at the pain.
I pulled with all my being!
Then lunged,
and bayoneted him again.
No word we spake.
No utterance he cried.
I stuck 'em once: I stuck 'em twice...

And then he died.

47) A Glass Before They Go

In hallowed halls,
Behind thickened walls,
The privileged
wine and dine.
They plot our fate,
Between the plates...
Of fish and fowl.
These modern-day
Parliamentarians who'd
Slit your throat...
To fill their purses.
So, still
they're sending loyal soldiers

To their deaths.

48) Bluff Cove

We arrived like thieves in the night.
The darkness cloaking us, hiding us,
Rendering us invisible.
We swarmed over the land,
Making it ours.
The smoke rising from the chimney.
Chinks of light,
split the night like laser beams.
While inside the building a young boy closed his eyes.
By the light of his cake's flickering candles he blew.
With a slight tap on the door,

we made his wish come true.

49) Class of 1982

The ground trembled, as they passed.
Softly sung words, bugle calls and pipes,
Which once again
Woke us from our slumber.
Revived our spirit,
So we too joined.
Sat upon those steps
At the entrance
To Valhalla.
That bond
That only warriors share
Made light that day,
The joyous celebration
Of our deeds
30 Years gone
But never a day forgotten.
The silence has returned
as has the birdsong

Now ceased their laments

50) Unbekannter Englisher Soldat...

I met, a fellow paratrooper
While I was on the road.
And I stopped there, for a chat.
Perhaps a chance, to reload.
And I could see...
that I'd be safe,
For British Airborne...
Now,
Held this place.
Both, above... And, below...
As I cleaned my rifle,
I wondered.
'Neath that crude cross...
Who lies there now?
I only know, 'tis a soldier...
With, no name.
But known to God.
And all I know.
He...
Is

My Brother ...

51) We'll Always Hear

From stormy desert winds,
I hear, the sound... of battle's roar.
The rattle, and, the chink of link.
As death, sweeps... the desert floor.
Followed by...
the crump, of the mortar, and the shell.
Welcome to my world...
On the battlefield of hell!
The wind, like the noise...
Is now, abated.
Dawn... filters through, another... sleepless night.
When we've formed,
and stood... upon that wall.
We'll always hear...

That wind!!!

52) Say My Name, Meet Me In...

The RED has changed to GREEN
And we're heading out the door!
While...
Invisible hands, pluck at me,
As I plummet.
Seeking... the van of battle,
in this fucked up war.
While the music in my head...
has turned into a ROAR!
And I have no thoughts, other,
Than victory...
or,

Valhalla...

53) Mines...

Pink Mist...
They may have gone,
But their legacy remains.
...Prosthetic limbs and death!
No dissemination of age,
Gender colour or creed.
Man nor beast...
Soldier or civilian.
Mines... .

Out there.

54) I'm On the Road to

You, with your neat picket fence
And freshly mown lawn.
Where only the occasional daisy
Pokes through.
Sedately content
You survey your domain.
While I, ignored by the passing thrall
I sit on this dusty plain
My withered limbs
Say it all
Too sick to move
I await Kismet.

As far as the eye can see
Caught in the dying sun's rays
The glint and glitter
Of the death that surrounds me
Thousands of miles away
You decide my fate.
'Tis not gold that's a lying
But the brass casings
Left in pitiful piles
From the lead that's been flying
Too scared to close my eyes
Should I not wake.

The sky fills with death
While the ground trembles
No trace they'll find
Of my insignificant bones
Ramadan's done
'Tis the time of Christ.
All this
While you reach for your morning coffee.
As I lay dying

On the road to Kandahar

55) Death Lingers.

That smell of death,
It hides around the corner.
The next fold in the ground,
That hill in the distance.
It mocks you,
Eggs you on.
Laughs at your fears,
Invades your mind.
Death taunts you,
Makes you think irrationally.
Tests your skills,
Hides from your reason.
Beyond your tangible grasp,
Gone in a split second.
But still there,

Always.

56) All Our Tomorrows

WE,
now see.
For those who lie where they are fallen.
We,
are their hopes,
their dreams.

Our,
thoughts keep them alive.
To die alone far from home,
no loved ones near.

We,
feel their pain,
now live their anguish.

We knew them all.

Speak no ill of the dead.

Scholar,
Fool, or
Pisshead.

I knew them all,
and all knew me.

57) *Lament of the Dead.*

What if I should die before the dawn?
And if I should die before the dawn,
What news ho, of me in England?
How cry you now?
Oh, men of mice!
Safe last night you slept.
'Twas the wind of war,
Wot kept me awake.
How say you now friend,
Did we win?

That some sad price was paid
For the laughter of today
That they should not forget.
But never know
The ignominy
Of death
While in their moments of play.
Brave men died
Tho' thousands of miles away
The same sun shone on both.

58) The Road is Long...

My friends.
Do not think of me, and weep.
For I'm not gone, I merely sleep.
...I see you all, as you see me.
A youth, and in my prime, carefree.
Until... again we meet.
Raise for me a glass then,
And from it, drink deep.
There I'll meet you in your dreams.
As a lover, friend or brother.
Before again, I search out.
The warrior's path... that leads,

To Valhalla!

59) The Gully Was Dead

I stood, within those ranks.
I fought, within that foe.
I saw them run, I saw them fall!
Some got up.
But not them all...
While yellow gorse, crackled,
... as it burned.
Its greyish smoke...
did claw,
And ravaged, all our throats.
The wind changed,
The flames moved on...
But not us...
We stayed!
We'd fought hard...
and knew... we'd earned.
This piece... of,

ground.

60) For Those That Man That Wall

And...
If... you believe, in God.
Say a little prayer... for me.
Forgotten, by the masses.
I'm forgotten, by... All.
Missed... by a mere minority!
On foreign shores, is where I be.
Unloved, feared.
Surrounded, by... the enemy.
Who wants,
... to kill me!
And they will never, have their fill
... of death!
I stand with my brothers,
Shoulder to shoulder...
A human wall.
We stand against...
Alone,
We stand

Against that evil thrall.

61) There's Not Many Left, to...

I smile, that knowing smile.
That only those... that know.
Of them, that's been.
Of all, they've seen.
That's those, that's lived,
Who now

tell... the tale.

62) Raise A Glass, Sing And Dance

For...
September's here, once more.
And every year remembered, since... 44.
From the sky, they came.
Met the earth...
Where they, then... remained.
Young men, mere boys.
Now caste, as warriors...
They met, "Valhalla's" call.
They fought, some died...
... They gave it...
Their all.

At a place called Arnhem

63) Tranquillity

No fear of dying.
We are... immortals!
Our death's, already, begun.
Soldiers of St Michael...
Airborne, everyone!
No love, to share.
No one, to care.
Just war, beer...

And death

64) It's a Brotherhood...

 I think, sometimes... there,
Are those of us
Who have... a philosophical,
View of fate.
An over acceptance... of
Que sera, sera.
Because, of what... we've done.
An empathy, with those...
that die,
Or whom, we... have killed.
Having previously been
one of his disciples.
Squires, of the "four horsemen".
Being...
A deliverer
...of pain,
...and

Of death!

65) Late... Again, Tell Me

I'd missed...
Roll call
This morning.
I wasn't there, I wasn't where...
I should have been.
And although... he called,
My name.
I never heard...
Not... this time.
Seems...
I'd missed...
Death's parade...
Once

More.

66) In War and...

I remember, when...
They were only made,
Of... paper.
And people, called them... weeds.
Quoted only in poetry.
Smoked... and grown,
Merely... for their seed.
Now worn...
With enamel, and...
glittery shiny bits.
A simple little flower...
The humble poppy
Which shows... our,
Sacrifice... worn now...
As a symbol...
of our

peace.

67) He's Somewhere Out There

Unmoving, still... like stone.
He kept his silent vigil
He stagged on... all alone.
His mucker's... laying close... beside him!
The darkness is their friend.
Cradling the swift scope
While dossing on the ground.
Half an hour till... stand to.
It's an hour till dawn.
Somewhere
A British army sniper,
Is stagging on...
With his mucker!

68) Travelling Companions On

The road to nowhere.
Death,
Whispered to me.
And we made... a pact.
To share a date.
And until then...
We shared a glass.
And had, one
For...

The road.

69) Battle Cry...

Mere men.
Mortals...
But sent by the Gods!
Warriors...
from the Sky.
At Hell's portal
They fearlessly fight,
And die!
Against all odds,
They take the ground...
Secure the day.
Forgotten, save by the few.
Their lives, they gave...
For you.

Wahoo Mohammed!

70) 2 Para, June 82... on,

It was some show...
Better, than Dante's inferno.
Bright colours...
Filled the night, as...
Death... filled the air
With a living, screaming rainbow!
Swathes of fiery light plucked,
Holes, in mortal souls.
While banshees'... eerie cries!
Heralded the end, for some.
While Paratroopers fought.
As shells and bombs rained down.
Some... were just thrown aside,
tossed... in the air.
To land and lie, and briefly laugh...
Before rising up,
to join in death's dance, once more.
And as suddenly as it began,
Once more Silence... filled the land,
as dawn, begun to break.
For the Valkyries...
had filled their quota.
On yon... last
vista...
Way down south!
Just before Stanley, at a place...
Called

Wireless Ridge.

71) A Bugle Called To

Signal them.
A simple, soulful, sound, that...
echoes... through lonely, trees.
A minute, of silence...
That lasts, eternal.
Remember them...
Of

Me

72) A Field Of

To all, it's known as...
The field.
At first, we were living in...
The field.
Then we were fighting on,
The field... of battle.
And before we knew it,
We were dying... in that field.
To all that saw it... to those, who were there.
It's a field... that remains, forever.
In, our

Dreams.

73) As He Loaded His Ammo

The brass was oily...
Slippery, to the touch.
But his hands... were cold !
And he was in rush...
Methodically, mechanically.
Into the magazines,
Coloured pieces of death... clicked.
As... the rounds were fed.
28, 29, last one... 30, mag filled.
Quick check... a push with his thumb.
Quick tap... on the palm.
Finally.
Another quick check...
He nudged the leg...
with his boot...
As the body was still warm.
But only

Dead eyes stared back.

74) They Fired

Little puffs...
of black, and white smoke.
Overhead.
Followed by crazy...
Catherine Wheel... like whizzing.
It signalled the arrival.
Of the... enemy's shells.
Set to explode... in the air,
and rain death...

upon us.

75) Do Bayonets Glisten Before You

Zzzzzzzzzzit!
Zzzzzzzzzzit!
Zzzzzzzzzzit!
Slow... and rhythmic.
As the steel... slowly fed,
The sharpening stone.
And eventually...
It began shine.
Along a fine...
Thin, line.
Where tapered steel
Now had an edge.
To cut and slash,
As well as...

Stab.

76) The Lull...

We sat in the gorse.
Smoking our cigarettes,
Whilst all around us
The gorse smoked too!

Flames flickered whilst
Branches crackled.
All the while
The shells rained down.

As the whitish grey smoke
Spiralled upwards,
Mingling
With their tobacco smoke

Small puddles,
Filled with brackish water
Reflected tired green men,
Now battle hardened.

77) Just Numbers

One tracer 4 ball
One tracer 4 ball
The chink of the link,
The roar as they fall.

Switch to the left,
Then switch to the right.
A cacophony of death,
Cut a swathe of fiery light.

One in Four,
Seven point, six two.
The sum total of life,
In that summer, of 82.

78) Telephone

The Chinook flew,
With us and its crew.
Four,
Plus eighty-nine.

All because,
The voice on the phone.
Said we're all alone,
And had been, for some time.

79) Most Attacks Were At Night

Tracer danced across the skies
Red, green, and white
Arcing, dipping, bouncing back up into the night.
Schumulies whizzed and 2-inchers plopped.
Star shells screamed to make you stop.
Flames in the gorse,
With smoke in your throat
Your feet splash through puddles
As you try to keep in line.
Hoping to find some cover.
Knowing,
there was no chance of finding sanity.
Confusion and shouting
Head for the voice
Don't bunch up, though often no choice.
Questions! Questions! Questions!
Do you know where we are?
Do you have any link?
Where's the fire support?
How soon till dawn?

Most attacks were at night.

80) Have You Seen

Have you seen a man die?
Do you know what it's like?
To see a man die.
To sit there together,
unable to help.

Do you know what it's like,
to watch a man die?
To hear that long,
last,
deep sigh.

Have you felt that emptiness?
What you can't describe.
Only, if you've been there,
can you know.
Did you cry?

Have you seen?
Do you know what it's like?
As he died,
did a piece of you?
Have you seen a man die?

Author's Notes/Comments:
I hope that nobody would be in this situation. It was hard
enough as a professional soldier, watching comrades who
had accepted their fate suffer.

81) The Thirty-Yard Dash

If he makes thirty yards
I'll get up and go.
Up and running
Jigging to and fro.

If he makes forty yards
I'll get up and go.
Is it your fear,
That seems to make him run so slow?

Go boy! Go!
If he makes another ten yards.
I'll get up and go.
Run boy, go! go! go!

Then you're there.
You're up and running.
If I make thirty yards.
Laughing as I go!

You move so slow.
If I make thirty yards.
And if I don't,
Will I ever Know?

Author's Notes/Comments:
I was that soldier.
Coronation Point, Falkland Islands, 1982.
Machine gunners from hidden trenches opened up on us.
It happened like it says in the poem.

82) Going Ashore

It was cold,
it took your breath away,
it was bloody deep.
It came to just under my arms,
I'm six-two.
It was twenty metres of ice-cold,
inky black,
ball-shrinking hell.
That bastard behind me,
poking me,
knocking me off balance,
kicking the back of my legs,
a total pain in the arse.
He was next.
I started to giggle,
Not such a bad day after all.
He was only,
five foot.

83) Goat Ridge

We huddled together,
while the shrapnel bounced off the rocks.
Waiting for the generals to make up their minds.
Cup of tea sir?
Would you like a bit of scoff?

84) Why

I've walked the leafy lanes of England.
Climbed the daunting mountains of Wales.
I've sat cramped in Irish darkness,
whilst my Scots blood boiled.

I've lived like a cowboy, on the North American
plains.
Drank for tomorrow, and the day after that.
I've listened to the rain as it crashed on tropical trees.
Tipped sand from my boots, while the sun browned
my knees.

No shit, that's the motto.
No dead, no wounded.
Jungle rules apply.
Duty fighter front and centre.

Not for flags.
Nor Kings.
Not for Queen.
Nor country.

It's for your mates.

85) *I'm better than he,*

Better kit,
Better trained,
Better fed,
Better led.
I'm better than he.
I'm a professional.
A MERE conscript is he.
No specialised training, no mission in life.
Mother, father, sister, perhaps a wife.
I'm better than he.

To the death then.
For this pile of sheep's dung.
All for the woman with the Tory blue rinse.
The smoke fills your lungs.
The whistling shrieks, fill your ears.
I'm better than he.
You scurry forward, under covering fire,
The lifeless eyes see not as you go.
I was better than he.
Death has no second best.

But was he really the foe?

86) Love, Lust & Death

The blue of the sea,
Will always be precious to me.
As is the pale of the sky,
For in the respite.
I breathe deep and sigh.
Before the nightly tracer splits the sky.

I remember the times that we had,
Wanton.
Drunken, and lustful.
With no tomorrows.
Could you visit me in my dreams?
Should I fall asleep for awhile?

Could I perish in the night?
Would that memory keep?
Should I die?
Too many questions do I ask.
Will the angels bring us together?
Or will I forever remain

in this land near the pole.

87) The Survivor

You feel bad, so you have a little drink.
Another makes you feel better.
Several more makes you feel great.
The devil's the barman
Hell's today, purgatory's tomorrow
Grey steel, black nights
The stars remain the same.
Eight thousand miles away,
They lie in their beds.
Dreams forgotten, ambitions
unfulfilled.
Integrity, honour, and freedom.
Politicians' words,
For a soldier's trade

is Death.

Sometimes I feel that the government let us down.

88) Letters From The...

I got a bluey...
on a mountain.
All the way... from home.
And I wondered if...
should I read it now...?
Or wait, until tomorrow?
What words, may it contain?
I fancied... I could smell...
In a lover's fair hand.
Your scent... upon the ink.
All the while
I'm sitting in a muddy hole 8,000 miles away...
Where I viewed
A vista unsurpassed!
Where I saw stricken ships... sink.
And wrapped... within
a simple sheet... of paper!
Within my pocket,
Lay...
My

Heart.

89) *Not By Bread*

Energy in the form of...
Little grey swirls,
Brushed aside the grass.
Coppery messages,
from...
Death.
They passed me by.
Drawing fragments, of my soul.
Sucked by the bullets' wake.
My fear, for a moment gone.
Until, we rose, to fight.
And I stood...

Alone.

90) *Ah... Proximity.*

A nearness,
A time.
A fuse... for H.E.
A means of death.
When shared with...
White phosphorous... it's,
Salt 'n' Pepper.
But mainly... it's,

Death and destruction.

91) The Smoke At...

A plume... of smoke.
Rising...
Behind the outcrop,
... as black... as,
The ace of spades.
The card of... death!
It drifted, no, it spewed... upwards.
Stark... chilling.
More... than just smoke.
It rose,
like...
A malevolent genie.
Against a serene... blue sky.
A bad omen...
for what, was yet to come.
On that day, the 6th of June,
82...
Where two knights lay at anchor.
In that small harbour
Bluff Cove, near...

Fitzroy.

92) Just A Hill

Soggy smelling peat
On a smoke obscured hill,
Death,
like a blanket.
Souls bonded together,
fear conquered.
Haggard
pale pinched faces,
Only the eyes,
Bright, alert,
The mirror of our
souls.

93) I Listened For The Call, Which

I smelled the peat,
and it's foreign earth.
My fingers, clawed and,
buried deep.
And the world...
turned... upside down.
But, I held on...
While it all erupted.
Death... played his game!
And I waited... my turn.
Which...

Never came.

94) Relentless Was...

Inadvertently,
I caught Death's eye...
So I laughed him in the face!
In response...
He laughed his wicked laugh,
And with his breath he hissed.
Next time!!!
And then he carried on...

His slaughter.

95) On My Lips Was...

I cried out, in my pain...
But you weren't there.
I lay there, 'tween...
The swaying heather.
Below, that yellow gorse.
Lead, had burned me.
And it hurt me bad.
I called out quietly,
In a dying whisper...
I called

Your name.

96) They Split the...

They burn...
like, the colours... of, the rainbow.
Fiery... trails of death!
There is White,
Red and Green.
An Orange one too,
though... seldom seen.
While the Black and Grey... hardly see the light of
day.
Just like jelly beans.
I've used them all...
And more.
They lit up the sky...
They split the

Night.

97) The Dying Man

Cold.
Afraid and alone.
Lost in the blankets of darkness.
Life slowly seeps from the wounds.

Where now were my comrades?
Who would now comfort me?
I see my mother's face
Smell her sweet fragrance.

Her tender embrace,
Brings brief warmth.
But not for my body
Only my soul.

My life is nearly over
Before it has scant begun.
My hopes and aspirations
Ended on this dammed hill.

May 82.

98) *A Friend Has Passed This Way*

I too have seen,
and watched.
Oft at times, mayhap reflected!
Those sad, and tired eyes.
Wherein a grin, a craic,
Helps maintain the masquerade.
Those mirrors of our soul.
Lacklustre, shows.
Where shine,
and life's mischief's twinkle
Have now long gone.
Only captured...
By one who never lies!
That omnipresent lens.
Where demons snuff the sparkle,
To make you think you have no hope.
Leaving...
A conflict of the mind,
the soul,
the thirst of life.
A choice to quench the fire in your brain.
So finally there's peace.
But only for you...
A friend has passed this way

R.I.P. Steve "Hank" Hood
A Lover, A Husband, A Father and an Airborne
Soldier.
Forever Young Class of 82.

99) *Of Melancholy Rapture*

Be careful... as to where ye point
Yer finger... of blame!
Of what ye quote... and who ye name.
What stones get upturned...
Of lies that come to light.
Of what ye yearn.
For money, or mayhap the infamy...
of the spotlight's glare.
There's more than one my son,
Who knows the truth...
Coz we were there!
Please praise be to God.
And all just remember, it pays not.
... To fuck with the Dead!

Of Melancholy Rapture... No Doubt

100) *What I Miss Most*

I miss those crisp clear nights,
when the frost glistens in the moonlight.
I miss those lonely exposed hills,
lashed by the rain.
I miss the young and innocent faces,
some of whom we'll never see again.
I miss the laughter and the craic.
I miss their morbid humour,
the childish pranks and unspoken laws.
I miss the sense of belonging,
that unique bond.
I miss youth at its best,
though I'll grow old, unlike the rest.
What I miss most?

I miss the lads.

101) 3 Para

Men of the Airborne.
Tell them of the mountain!
Of three long days...
Of what we did.
Of dark, and bloody nights.
When death, passed amongst us
When fate, cast his die.
Where hell opened its gates.
On a cold and snowy June.
Of a forgotten war,
Near the bottom of the earth.
But not for us...
Sleep well my brothers.
Our mission's done.
We'll tell them of your deeds.
Of three days on a mountain,
In June.
Of… Paratroopers

Way back then.

102) Summer's Come...

Though it's
Blocked out the sun!
But, he wasn't looking anyway.
Roaring... filled ears.
Time slowed, then stopped.
While death flew,
...cleansing, the air.
Molten metal shards, pierced... clothes.
Then mortal flesh.
Indiscriminate, uncaring, unceasing.
It rolled like a tide, killing unmerciful.
Leaving nowhere to hide.

In the middle of June.

103) I Couldn't Cry So I…

The mist, parted… before me.
Swirled… around behind me.
Filled, the void… I'd created.
I strode through the night!
The mist, death… and me.
Hollow, eerie echoes…
for each, near silent… footfall.
Like a spectre from the past,
Lost souls willed me on.
Even more wished me ill...
and they all

Laughed.

104) I Ran Hard,

And…
I ran fast!
I dodged, to the left.
I zagged, to the right.
As the roar, filled… my ears.
Hot lead, split… the night.
My head went back,
and
my screams, became… a, strangled laugh!
Valkyries' wings fluttered
Copper flew, at 800 metres,
a second.
And
I ran,

Towards… death!

105) *A toast to my brethren.*

Lonely Planet...
I've choked on dust, driven...
by, swirling sand.
I've, tasted blood 'n' tears.
Mixed, with sweat, and the planet's mud.
I've had, my soul washed by...
Rain, sometimes so cold.
My heart froze!
Oft I went, where no man... had ever, been.
Where none, ever will again.
I've kissed, sweet lips...
And
I've met women, who...
in the morning.
Looked, rougher than... me.
I've stolen into ladies' hearts.
And then, crept from their beds.
With all said and done, and...
All, where I've been.
I still remain...
A

Lonely man...

106) Someday

I'll search out...
some forgotten wall,
and write my name,
upon it.
Amongst...
the other,
forgotten names...
where I'll remain,
forgotten.

Soon

107) That Scarlet, Flowers... Spread!

Where poppy seeds lay scattered.
From the muddy fields of, South Armagh...
... the snowy vistas, of the South Atlantic... or...
... upon the dusty, afghan plains.
Seeds trampled, by a British soldier's boot.
In that incandescent light, from falling flares.
Or the emstar's green and ghostly glow.
As Gympy tracer crisscrossed the night
I've seen death, take... its toll.
I heard the cries, of dying men, in the darkness down
below.
While the ground erupted,
and hell spewed forth... its shards of death.
As limbs dissolved,
in pink mists... of pain.
I'd seen a smiling lad...
Who'd never see, his loved ones, err again.
Now laying as a tangled mass
Of torn flesh, and broken bone.
Another name upon the wall.
Another sunset he'll not share, he's met his soldier's
fate.
For evil men and death conspired...
In the dark, before the dawn.
While politicians talked of peace.
Our brave men and women...
Died!
A thankless death

On foreign soil.

108) Vergessen

Only now, it's the birds that sing.
It's only, the dead, that... watch.
Though no longer hear.
For silence, fills their world.
As mud, now fills, my ears.
I lie, where I had fallen.
Near a trench, immersed in water, and filled with death.
Where birds, once pecked.
Feasted, on warm, and rotting flesh!
Immune, to the sound of the bullets, and the screaming shells.
Lifeless... limbs, hung on the wire.
Gently swaying, and...
beckoning, on the breeze.
To fall, flesh stripped.
Beneath, the tide of war, and...
Flanders mud.
100 years ago.
Where we still lie
Forgotten...

Forever to remain

109) No barriers,

No bounds,
No limitations,
By creed, colour, or by age...
A feeling, which is...
Invisible, to the naked eye.
Contentment... of which.
I seek no more.
As for which I once sought,
dreamed... and.
Lusted for.
Once, I dined on babies' heads.
Washed them down, with char, or screech.
And nasi goreng, sometimes...
hit the spot.
Though it was roast beef, and the pud I missed.
And French was a tongue.
I had to learn, come habitude.
And life
was much more, simple

then.

110) Last Battle For

The night,
Turned into grainy day.
As fingers of smoky light,
Drifted across the blackened sky.
While tracer... followed shadows,
The wind,
...brought screaming shells.
Death wreaked his havoc
Turned the landscape into hell.
We dug, we cut, we sliced.
Only the dead, stayed still.
We chased them up the slope
And over the top.
We chased them left to right .
We chased them... all the way, down...
To

Stanley.

111) Sun Ray's Down... Sun Ray's...

Follow me, boys.
And off he went…
Charging,
up that gully, disappearing…
Through… the smoke,
past the bodies…
Of Captains Wood, and Dent.
Low and fast, grim faced.
Weaving midst the burning gorse.
Onwards,
up Darwin hill… he raced.
To a rendezvous, with destiny… filled with death.
Where the fates had conspired.
Where he met… a hail of lead.
Where the enemy's guns,
cut him… down.
Stone

Dead.

112) Drum Roll For An

Just a blur…
But it was movement!
So he let rip…
Flashes, flecks… of light,
Staccato noises, burst the night.
The ground shook, with thunder.
Off they went, into the fray.
As the sun rose, while...
Bullets still flew.
Battle weary… paratroopers,
Sat, smoking,
Within… the, smoke.
And pondered, at our day.
We sat,
And waited…
For, the dark

Encore.

113) It's Been A...

On a jungle path.
I passed a jaguar...
taking a nap.
And in his sleep,
He winked at me!
While fire ants,
Searched... for food.
Up above monkeys,
chattered... as they rocked,
the trees.
As leaves crunched
underfoot.
And everything was brown, or
Green.
But if you brushed a bush!
You might have to...
Wait,

a while!

114) Half light... and

It's the last, wherein.
I'll see your face... Before the dawn.
No words, no sound... nothing...
'Cept a chilling death-like smile.
The air, is still, and I've held
my breath.
Silence pervades, and still no sound.
I blend, with night, I meld with nature.
Bidden by the figure with the scythe.
Eerily like ghosts, we rise...
From the cold, wet ground.
Shoulders hunched, moving low.
Onwards towards death ...
stealthily, we did go.
And nearly, we made it.
There's music, in the wind...
And a sadness, in my voice.
But I'll not speak, a word.
For it's a song, that I'll not sing.
I am, the living dead.
For my heart, is now made of stone.
I, no longer, hear... your words.
I...
No longer see

That deathly grin.

115) Freedom, Mere Mortals

Down in the valley,
Midst the purple heather,
The wind tickles, 'n' teases,
The golden gorse.
Therein lie, rusting remnants,
Hidden by, the long, yellow grass.
Like a battle's roar.
The rumble of thunder,
Swells and fills the land.
Prelude to a storm,
And a clash...
Of the gods.
Whilst in silent calm.
Those that remained,
Cast long shadows.
Silhouetted, by lightening.
Vigilantly they keep watch
From their slumbering graves

Having paid the price.

116) Dash, Down, Crawl, Or...

Muscle, sinew, tissue.
Determination, tenacity.
Pitted against...
Metal... bullets, molten fragments.
Shells 'n' grenades.
Living and the dead.
Fire and movement.
On the field of battle
We all talk to each other,
It's an indication!
That, you're either, one of the,
Living...
Or

You're dead!

117) Once Again...

I touched the earth.
I felt, its staccato beat.
She embraced me.
As I hugged... the dirt.
Fear, pushed me forward,
Though, not fear of death,
But...
Of dying alone.
Of being... dead,
All

By myself.

118) Not The Tunes of Glory, But

Climb on up here boy,
Sit beside me for a while.
And I'll tell you a story of my war,
Not a blood thirsty one, of
Deeds and senseless death.
But heart-warming ones.
Referring to acts of selfless glory.
Simple tales.
Of a group of men... that,
Simply went to war.
And saw all its horror.
That their deeds were,

So awe inspiring.
Their actions saved my life.
They so died, while I lived.
So now...
I'll teach you how to sing,

My Brothers' songs.

119) On the Roll...

Not every day!
But some...
I remember them.
And like yesterday,
We've talked and...
What's been said,
Has been done!
When all is said...
I've wished upon,
A crooked cross.
And said a prayer...
For some,

Of The Dead.

120) Hey! Be Sure and True...

Save me space... On the table.
In the great hall... in Valhalla!
Make sure there's grog aplenty.
Mead, wine, women, 'n' song!
For I've a thirst,
that will last a thousand years.
And a hunger that's, unconsumed.
I've left my true love's heart... behind.
For I have entered,
The Warriors' realm.
To be with

My brothers!

Class of 82

121) We'll Always Hear...

From stormy desert winds,
I hear the sound of battle's roar.
The rattle and, chink of link,
As death, sweeps, the desert floor.
Followed by the crump
Of the mortar, and the shell.
Welcome to my world...
On the battlefield of hell.
The wind, like the noise...
Is now abated.
Dawn filters through,
Another sleepless night.
When you've formed
and stood upon that wall.
We'll always hear...

That wind.

122) *War Wounds From*

My shoulder... burns.
Sometimes, it pains.
Was it the jump in Italy
In that river bed?
Or landing on those sandy
Sudanese deserts?
Mayhap an icy sleep on the
North American plain.
A result of a thrown brick,
On some policing action.
Trauma perhaps...
From a Falklands War.
Or just...
A drunken weekend,
In

Aldershot.

123) *Sybaritic, But I Promised not to Tell*

A sensuous pleasure... Perhaps if.
You were to catch me... if,
I'm smiling.
Or even, if... I'm blue!
Perhaps,
you want to share, a... tomorrow.
Or merely...
Just a moment... of my time.
For, right here, for, right now.
And if I got a kiss...
I promise

not to... tell.

124) I Whispered As

The darkness called.
And it's cries, echoed... in the night.
I'm cold.
No rest, for me.
The rhythmic beating, of... my heart
Is stilled
There's a, chill...
Upon, my soul.
It's a long time, since... I felt,
the wet sand, beneath...
bare feet.
Or a lover's subtle breath.
Upon
My lips.
There's a sadness in my eyes.
That's killed, the spark.
Life, withers...
For

Death, called out my name.

125) All the Colours of A Rainbow?

The scent of your love.
If I could, just transcend...
Those moments... to a colour.
It might be...
The colour, of your eyes,
Of a morning.
Or perhaps...
The colour, of your lips,
Of a moonlit evening.
Or,
The colour of... your blushes.
In moments of wanton... passion.
Which lingered like a rainbow.
But is all gone now!
Causing my eye to jade.
I no longer know the scent!
Am therefore, am rendered... .
colour blind.
As while I forlornly search,
for that lover's... litany.
And all the while I do...
My current colour, is...

A paler shade of Blue.

126) Could You Hear That...

A sound... so fine.
While I slept...
Winds howled,
As waves, smashed!
Upon, many different shores.
And around the world...
Guns roared, and people died.
But above it all...
Was it only I,
Who, heard...
That

A butterfly, was crying?

127) I Dream To

Life's full of dreams, where...
Childish dreams,
are meant to fade and die.
Impossible dreams,
are meant, to fail...
because we didn't try.
Our worst thought dreams...
Turn into nightmares!
Because love got in the way?
Or we never shared!
Or we cared...
Too

Much.

128) I'll Take It

It's your smile.
I truly, fell in love with!
Its wickedness, reflected...
In your eyes.
A pixie-like voice,
That could command.
Whilst, full of passion.
Didst...
Melt, a stony heart.
And caused, a tear... to dwell.
For all my life,
A regret, for all time.
A memory, of love.
To take...
To

My grave.

129) Hold Me as I Sleep, and Kiss Me

Just...
Make, sweet love... To me.
Teach me, to... dance!
Meet me... there.
Amongst, the stars!
Take my hand, and... steal my heart.
I, now have the keys... to,
the asylum.
And caused, a tear... to dwell.
So come, and set me free.
Just, share with me, for the moment.
Don't try to understand me.
Don't look too deep.
You won't like... what you see.
Keep the colours loud, and keep them bright.
Drown, reality,
in fizzy wine and froth.
All, I'm asking... of you,
Is...
Tell me, that you love me.
And, be there,
In the morning

When I awake.

130) I Kissed, a Myriad, of... Light

It's just...
How, to kill a wish!
Sometimes a wish, is so obscure.
It lays beyond, the realms, of fantasy.
So we no longer dream, of it... encore.
And once the spirit of love's verse is, lost...
I searched, within a memory.
For a dream.
And saw that girl, from the squat...
that played, the guitar,
so well.
Another... The barmaid...
Not forgetting the redhead, that shaved.
And I only knew...
the true colour of her hair,
because... she told me.
Long forgotten memories
That happened before, an epic... journey
I once made in life.
And could I ever forget, that...
Summer

in Bexley Heath?

131) The Fabric of Our Being, is...

A letter to Althea?
When I was in jail.
I wrote one similar, from the Traz.
But not four walls...
For one was full of bars.
I washed my clothes, in a sink.
I dried them, hanging
From, my windows...
And they never smelled, more sweeter!
Nor, we're any cleaner, than.
A free man's

Clothes.

132) Some Promises

Like, drops of rain.
Some run away.
Some form, puddles
Some, wash the tears...
From, your skin.
Others evaporate,
with the warmth, of the sun.
Whilst some fill, and drown...
your heart.
Or... maybe they just...
Disappear, in the ether.
But, still linger... in the mind.
Some wistful
Some

Too dark, to keep.

133) When

You've seen things,
beyond... the realm,
of reason.
Where, you've lived,
within... a,
twilight world.
Where a dream,
was once... reality.
Though not, necessarily,
a faerie tale.
When life,
no longer,
tastes... sweet.
Nor is, serene.
Fear no evil.
For, I have tread that path.
Spoke with death.
And

We whispered, dead men's words.

134) 70 Virginis...

The ocean, rocked... me.
As the waves, pushed me... towards,
the sandy shore.
I'd floated in on, the ebbing tide.
Drifting, on the water.
I'm floating on a sea of pain,
and abject misery.
Just staring, at the sky,
No longer, do I feel, the cold.
Nor hear, the crying of the gulls.
And I'm slowly sinking,
With despair.
In the Goldilocks Zone

Eyes... opened... wide.

135) *Did You Ever*

Kiss, a...
Wisp?
Or taste an exotic drink, they don't make, no more...
Or wish, there was more to life
Than just, foolish whims.
Sombre, are my thoughts.
While my memories, are... murky, black.
You were, that... tree,
full of, forbidden... fruit!
That was, so lush, once plucked.
I kept going back, for more.
Sweet, was the taste, of sin.
And so I ask...
Why?
And would I,
Ever

Know... ?

136) There Could Never Be...

Whence on rain-painted streets.
Under a waning moon and falling stars.
My life and dreams were... Shared.
Remembering,
the sparkle in your eyes.
The mischief, in your laugh,
and star shine... From your smile.
All, t'while... I'm missing,
the warmth, of your lips on...
Winter nights.
And how you held me tight.
'Tis no other's heartbeat, I wish to hear.
I long to pass each majik moment, like enchanted
lovers, caught in a pleach.
As I could never, share again...
With

... anyone but you!

137) 470 Nanometres, It's Just

If you know her...
Could you, pass this along, from me?
The nights, have grown darker, and... lonelier, now,
that you have gone.
I no longer see, a sparkle, in...
blue eyes.
With which, the twinkling, of the night's stars,
I did, once... compare.
The sky, it seems, has now, lost its lustre.
While, I have lost.
My
Lovely eyes...
Of

Blue.

138) Whisper...

My name.
Like, I once, whispered... yours.
In the dark, of the night,
while, holding... you close.
Or, when we were apart.
Or when, I felt the want, of your love.
I'll forever whisper your name.
When,
an Angel's feather, touches, my heart.
When I'm melancholy, and feeling lonely.
When I think, I can smell,
your... perfume.
Or I thought I heard your voice, upon the wind.
Your voice is embedded, in my soul.
So just...
Whisper

My name...

139) I No Longer Cast a Pebble, For

I heard the sadness, in your voice.
That showed me, the colour, of...
your soul.
And it matched, the purity...
of your eyes.
Oft, I hear, their... silent call.
And wonder...
Should I respond
Or just wait, my turn... ?
While in my eyes... there's
A deadness, to match.
The colour, of their shrouds.
There's a darkness, that...
Fills my heart.
To catch
Those

ripples on the pond.

140) The Devilled Bones Of

Woe...
The absence, of light.
Once again.
I'm drinking, on my own.
Waiting, for the darkness.
The whisper, of... wings.
Valkyries.
To claim, my soul.
To, take me home.
We're having, a party.
Just me,
'n'

... the dead.

141) Sadness

Rules, my soul.
While my heart, lays waning.
I miss each touch, and every kiss.
And still, my body... lays, wanting.
Love.
Never, more... I'll be.
Not, once more, will I see.
And while my lips, crack, and chafe.
In dreams.
I only think, of those, long... dead.
'N' kiss, lost... forgotten lovers.
Only ever thinking, of the past.
So my wish, is not... to dream.
For my past is my future.
And, so it... remains.
Tomorrow, will be, yesterday...
While today, will ever be,
The day preceding... My death.
While an emotion

Stole my soul...

142). Today it's

Rain...
It rained.
And rained.
And rained.
And it's still

Raining

143) In Quiet Moments, There's Times

Deep, deep, down...
Beyond, where I think, and I can see.
Where lies a memory,
That haunts, my tears.
And, every now, and when
For some unknown... reason.
One, escapes my eye, and flows.
And sadness fills me.
For, I know... not.
Why

I cry...

144) Send Me

Flowers,
For... I love.
Their vibrant colours, and
Their, sweet, scent.
For, I miss my love,
and, the colours...
She didst bring!
And just like her, they'll not long, last.
But, a brief beauty...
Full of life, before they wilt,
and die
But, while they're here.
They'll, be... mine!
My tears, are real.
But my dreams, are made... of, smoke!
Which have dissipated, in the wind.
Like a fallen rainbow.
Like the discarded petals.
Of, my now...
Dead

Flowers

145) The Setting Sun

Melds the horizon.
As, moistened eyes, now mist my vision.
I've forgotten, most... of what I've seen.
While daylight hints, of fresh delights.
'Tis the darkness of the night.
Whose sombre song...
Reeks, death's melodious, tones.
To steal away...
Souls...

Before the dawn!

146) I Once Tasted...

Freedom, long ago.
And...
It was sweet, and like, no... other.
'Cept, perhaps, that... of love.
Though...
Now not for me... I'll no longer seek that spice
of life.
It brings no joy.
For it left bitter, splenetic reminder.
A taint, that spoiled fruit, doth sometimes have.
That permeates a soul.

And...

147) I've Heard It...

When a dead man, sings.
And it's sweeter, than...
Life itself.
Where time,
Has no limits, nor... conceptions.
When music, fills, my... being.
Let the music, move you,
Like it, sways... my soul!
There is no glory, in dying.
There never has, and never will!
So live today,
Like, there's... no tomorrow.
Live it wild, and
Live it

Loud... !

148) Love Might Touch

But not
When you're dead.
For when you're dead,
You've left, pain behind.
The colours, all, gone.
'Cept... black.
The black, will always, remain.
I've been left, all... alone.
Searching, for that someone.
Who's, somewhere.
Who's been absorbed, by the night.
Beyond the vision of my sight.
And thus, is rendered invisible.
To

My heart...

149) Edvard Munch

Once done a painting.
That, depicted... it well.
The "Silent Scream".
That came... from hell!
All seeing, non-hearing,
He knew my world.
He... knew it... well.
My scrawl of words,
From within... a dream.
Like Edvard Munch,
And

His scream.

150) I Walked the World and Now I'll

Remember the four continents, where...
I've stepped in grizzly bear shit...
Watched, a penguin...
Have a piss.
Seen...
Skies so clear
I could touch, the stars at night.
Felt a monsoon's rain...
As it Cleansed the streets,
Saw raindrops... turn to steam.
Watched fields, turn back
to mud, once again.
I've crossed dusty desert plains.
Ate jungle snake!
Drank...
Where dusky-eyed maidens...
Waved, and smiled,
with an... Innocence .
Which belied their years,
And their trade.
I've seen the world,
From an inverted... vertical, terminal dive.
Smoked 'em down... dumped it low.
Watched the red...
... and done the green!
Watched horizons disappear
Felt the earth... Move!
But I've always managed,
To

Walk away.

151) My Eyes Are Teeming

Don't speak to me
of
Tomorrows
Nor mention, the things...
I've done, for... love!
Sometimes, it's hard
To follow one's heart.
For, we don't always get...
to, choose...
Our moments.
And all my dreams, now...
lie in ruins.
When I hear your voice, I die inside.
Don't look at me, like... I'm
a fool.
For though it's only, mere... emotion.
I have a talent, to make those I love... cry!
Devotion... has destroyed my life.
Distance, it is said...
Makes the heart grow fonder, but it also ages, and...
fills it

with dust.

152) Death Led The Chant

So
Here's to dead men, everywhere...
Those, I know.
And those I don't... !
A small reminder, of those who've passed.
Like the sensation
It might cause in your eyes.
To burn... to see.
Of a past, resplendent.
Of an irritable tear.
Of a what if...
Of a time, we danced.
Of a time, the gimpies roared.
And 81 was a round, and not a year.
When millimetres, were in the hundreds.
And they filled the air
When death stalked, silent dreams.
We, walked amongst it.
We breathed, the air.
We stared death, in the eyes.
A Beyoncé of life.
Where, we never felt, the threat...
of death
Where we stood together.
And, history roared.
And, he may have touched me.
And, I remain scarred.

But he never stole my soul...

153) Of Marble Stone, Copper, 'n'
Lead, and

Once,
I was a tool of death.
A skill, I've learned, forevermore.
And so does, yet, still remain.
I've kissed, the blade.
I've pledged, my troth,
to...
God, the devil, 'n'... death!
I'm, too sad for slumber.
I'm too, lonely to sleep.
I can't rid my head,
of, that pervading scent...
Of... what the darkness brings...
A, prelude... to death!
And its stench, has filled the air.
Its sweetly, sickly perfume.
That lingers.
That's reminiscent...
Of rotting flesh, of corpses.
Of the expiration of life.
Of a smell...
Of

dead flowers.

154) The Rhythmic, Sinuous Wandering

of

A forgotten warrior.
And if...
I could trade, my taste of death
For the unspoken, thirst, of life...
Had I not, already drank, your aura.
And thus, knew, that I was doomed.
I'm keeping to the shadows.
At the setting, of the sun.
Silently, whistling, death's... bloody, intro.
An old man, wandering... lonely.
For we'd once met, and,
we'd...
Once, sang a song.
Death, like this man,
Meanders... on his way.
Seeking out, mammalians.
'Twas words, not deeds, that.
Stopped

My heart...

155) Where I've Been, I've Left my Mark

Though not, always, intentionally.
More like...
some wayward, puppy dog.
And on my travels,
I've breathed the mystic airs, of the east.
Tasted dreams, and fed from myth.
My beliefs ingrained, and...
my thoughts are, that...
I want to live for ever.
I've drank with legends
I've slept with those that, would
have me.
And for some... I've paid
For the pleasure.
I've fought in wars, with warriors.
And fought in bars

with drunken brothers.

156) I've Suffered the Wrath of

Love's demons.
I've been chased... Hunted.
Like a dragon.
I've fallen, from the sky...
Like a, bad... angel.
Passion
I've smelled its scent, upon the wind.
Its petals, scattered... trodden, underfoot.
I've stripped, the flowers... from,
the field.
I've bared, my soul... torn and, bloodied.
I've been schooled, in all the arts.
Qualified
To fight, to survive, to... kill.
On the path... Along, the way.
Destroying the beauty, of the planet.
... All
... ...the while.
My life's goal of...
Eliminating the enemy...
Killing,
my fellow

man.

157) When Life's...

Wine, has lost, its... sweetness.
When, a jejune horse, appears,
As it comes, upon the dawn.
I'll be in that group of four.
My last chance, at love... Then.
For,
I'd rather smell, a rose's scent.
Than that, of death, or fear.
And if you should you share, a kiss...
That'd melt, a dragon's heart.
Perhaps one last time.
Before, you stretch... your wings.
Before, a feather... falls.
And if not...
Take me now
For
My heart is lost.
My life

no longer a pleasure.

158) Roast, My Bones...

Then,
Scatter the ash.
Let the wind, take me,
To where, the Rhopalocera gather.
And they, will kiss me, with
their wings.
Their touch, filled, with...
All the colours of, the rainbow.
Held together, with... faerie dust.
And dragon's breath, will cast, a... shadow.
To engulf, my world,
And turn it

Black...

159) Here's Saying Goodbye

Draw me, a wish,
'Pon... a whitened wall.
Where words are, clear 'n' strong.
Rock me... a lullaby.
My children, will sing.
Colour me, a value.
That will last, after I'm gone.
Paint for me... a dream...
For I am,
Blind

To it all.

160) Farewell Goodbye...

I don't wish, an angel to,
Speak for me!
No polka dot shirt for clarity,
No obsolete dreams...
No test of destiny...
I'll meet your expectations,
With a smile and a curse.
My life has piqued!
And for that...
I wish you

Adieu

161) Emotions, Nil By Mouth, Nor Any Passed...

Within the darkness,
You were my light.
And now...
I'll dream, and, not... know.
Alcohol, fuelled thoughts.
That turn to dust, spread, on the wind.
Though, no mere squall, is this...
for Coriolis, has spoken.
What, with the dawn, remains... still fresh?
Or muddied by, a forgotten taste.
'Twas you, who said goodbye.
But by deed, and...
Not

By word...

162) *Have You Ever Seen*

If I told a story... Who would listen?
Would it be...
Of sugar 'n' spice, and all things nice.
Or doom n gloom,
blood tears,
'n' death ?
I've kissed beauty, at its best.
I've kissed the clouds, and,
the broken earth.
But... the sweetest kiss, was yours.
I used to drink, for the craic!
And the madness, that it brought.
The places that I saw and where I'd been... Lost
within a haze of drink.
Then came, a call to war.
And it all, did change.
I'd never longed, for the sun upon my face, before.
Now it brings back memories, of a childhood past.
You can shrug your shoulders, and sigh.
But the thoughts within your head, will still... remain.
Just who, exactly...
sees

the dead man's smile...?

163) I Am There

No time... to dream,
My time... is short.
The young...
the naive... the innocent.
Have gone to sleep.
I know the night...
As darkness envelops,
Suppresses all.
While I stay and linger.
I hold back their fears.
Soothe their brow,
Brush away their tears.
For those I love.

Always and forever.

164) Jekyll 'n'...

What lies within...?
What lays beneath,
That face you paint?
Does it mask...
Your pain?
Does it go beyond,
Your eyes?
Does it go deep...
within forbidden depths?
Does it sear your brain?
From whom, do you feel...
You have to...

... hide?

165) Moralistically Or...

How do you,
comprehend a message,
If the meaning is unclear?
Where dead men,
Tell no tales!
And no meaning is...
Intact.
Sufficed to say.
Do not doubt,
My...

Integrity.

166) Who's Knocking...

I sat drunkenly singing,
Upon a smoky black beach.
One tropical evening.
Mundy snored,
While the sea met the sand.
And I cursed Leedham!
Who had the key for...

Our door.

R&R Penang 1974

167) Never Leave a Man...

As oft as naught.
There's none that spares,
A thought.
Of babes at mother's breast,
Or curled round their feet.
Life goes on...
Though one has ended.
Forget not the strong,
The wives, mothers, lovers.
Who have been left...

behind?

168) In The Army It's

Shoulder to shoulder!
Shoulders to cry on.
Shoulder... arms

Shoulders back!

169) We're Soldiers, We Fight Wars

I saw brave men die.
Others wounded...
Suffered the horrors that are war.
We don't have much,
But do have pride.
We fought, we suffered,
some died.
For politicians...
Who now are rich!
While we...
We sell our bits of tin sir...
To get by,

That's what we do!

170) He Missed Me, But Not...

Death's camped,
outside my door.
For he's missed me,
once or twice before...
So now he lies in wait,
and I know this time
He's got another chance
And he's going to make sure!
I think I hear him calling...
It preys upon my mind.
His evil prescience is forever
He's trying to wear me down.
Methinks... he's not that bad,
He's the bringer of dreams...
after all.
At least he'll let me sleep
And reunite once again,
with...

   My mates.

171) The "Ghost"

Empathetic waves,
From a silver surfer.
Holding fast.
Riding...
beyond the graves.
Spread the word,
Let's have some fun!
Odin's got another warrior...
His time on earth is done.
Pete Harvey...

Is gone.

172) If Not For Mates...

I could have been,
lots of things in life.
But I wasn't!
I was a soldier...
A tool for the government.
A street cleaner, a fireman,
a world policeman.
A pawn in world peace.
A fixture, for the wrath...
Of everybody that could,
Throw a stone!
Could make a bomb...
Or had a gun.
And I stood and took it!
Though not alone .

But for the grace of God.

173) Somewhere...

Deep in A Foreign Country...
Several lyricals were waxed,
Neath, swinging, smoking lamps!
While sand bags leaked...
Mess tins boiled.
Brews were shared,
And...

We all... Stagged on!!!

174) A Clarity of Mind

There is a clarity of mind.
For those who have met death,
Stared him in the face.

Perspective,
Perceptions,
The meaning of life.

Inhumanity.
Suffering,
And strife.

Why I'm here.
You're here,
Why we live

Or why we die.

175) Tabbing

We tabbed,
And we tabbed.
We tabbed
For fucking miles!

The sun rose then set.
The moon came out.
On we tabbed.
Tabbing.

We stopped,
We fought!
We tabbed on.
For we were... mere

Men at War.

T.A.B.
Tactical Advance to Battle

176) Yesterday and Tomorrow

I have no voice for lullabies.
My tenderness,
Will always lay...
In my sweet caress.
And of moments when,
As you slept... I visited you.
While I brushed away...
Your silent tears.
I slew that magic dragon,
And from all your fears.
Released you.

For today I gave.

177) All Alone Just...

I'm in an empty room,
Where forgotten echoes ring.
And memories fade to grey.
I have made sacrifice.
Though who, has seen?
My rewards... but given to a few.
And even then,
None shall know.
'Cept God... and

Me.

178) The Battles Roar...

And in some eyes,
I saw real fear.
In others...
Simple resignation.
But still they went!

Off up the gully,
into the smoke.
Upwards,
and onwards,
towards the top.

Where they were met,
By Death!
Mere grams,
of copper and lead.
Struck them all down,

dead.

British Lions
Class of 82

Darwin Hill

179) Life's Dance...

Follow the crowd...
And if I were willing?
If you catch my drift.
Would I happily go along,
Put some sky beneath my feet...
Would I even join that throng
'N' just head off that cliff?
Or are we just all, after all...
Muroidea?
It's an excuse me it seems... it's the

Dance of the Lemmings!

180) As-salamu Alaykum

Ice has formed, on his shemagh.
While vapours from his breath,
Form miniature clouds, in the night,
Floating upwards, to the stars.
Just another day, like yesterday,
And how, it will be tomorrow...
Bluey black, in the moonlight.
The barrel of his weapon glints,
Its metal cold, to the touch.
Though strangely comforting...
Not long till dawn.
Soon there will be the call,
To prayer.

Wa Alaykum As-Salam.

181) Earth, Wind and...

Let the earth's thunder.
Drown out your...
Drums of war.
Let the chilling rain,
Soothe and cleanse...
Wash away the pain.
Look me in the eye?
Oh warrior from the sky.
When you have gone,
Retribution... will return,
Once more!
Know now your comrades...
Died... for nothing!
On this far, and distant shore.
For we fight a holy war!
And our bones turn to dust.
That on the wind... chokes you.
Oh warriors of the sky.
My soul is black, like the night.
But my eyes burn,
With a martyr's...

Fire.

182) Remember

I have nothing left to offer you,
Merely words,
of which I have an abundance.
My wealth,
is of an experience.
Which now lies within my past
Of those far-off shores.
Of the men,
Of the Class of 82.

So come hear my words
Of deeds and men.
Tales not oft told?
But remembered by that few.
To who we raise glass,
Of what men did,
Before you were.
To those men,
Of

The Class of 82.

183) It Blew In From... ..?

It was an icy chill,
That crept in,
Long before the snow fell.
Deep, in his bones it went.
Slowly...
encompassing, his heart.
Then his soul!
It weighed him down,
stopped his thoughts.
Ended his existence.
A wind?
He never knew.

It just... blew.

184) Colder Than Paradise.

I don't cry so much now.
Perhaps, all my tears are gone?
Perhaps, the snow has frozen them?
Perhaps... Who knows,

just Perhaps.

185) Let Us Sleep

Oh!
You, selfish bastards.
So young, insolent.
Who would
Disturb,
Our eternal slumber.
Would spoil,
Our hard won
Sleep.

We.
Some, not all.
Once
Though still now,
Younger than
You.
Unnamed we lie
Forgotten,
Save the Few.

We
For, an eternity
Slept
Beneath the loam,
Our battlefield
Peaceful
Come join us
Or,
Leave us be.

Again
That, foreign call
'Tis
Life's unjust travesty,
Worldly conflict
Waste.
England's sovereign soil
God,
Save the Queen.

186) H

All colours gone, only the grey.
The face,
in the cold light of day.
Down off that hill.
To the rows of the dead,
awaiting below.
The face,
in the cold light of day.

It was the last time I saw him.

Author's Notes/Comments:
Col. H Jones 2 Para 1982. I saw him before, and
during the battle for Darwin Hill. I helped to carry his
body down to the RAP at the rear of Darwin Hill. It
is how I remember him.

187) Sapper Hill

The granite was cold,
While the yellow and white lichen scraped the skin.
But the view was magnificent.
To the left the sea,
placid blue.

The red and green coloured roofs
which contoured along its shores.
Likened to an artist's upturned paint box.
Splashing colour,
over the otherwise bland yellow landscape.

To the right Sapper Hill,
the main focus of attention.
Where 'neath the small puffs of black and white smoke,
The black ant-like figures scurried,
to and fro.

The lone helicopter's arrival signalled the end.
We had watched in small dispassionate groups,
whilst death had rained down before us.
There being apparently,
a fine line between attrition and slaughter.

Helmets off, berets on.
We moved down the ridge into the valley.
Towards Stanley.

Author's Notes/Comments:
14/15 June 1982. End of a war.

188) Remember Me?

Cherry lips
Whose sweet caress,
I miss your touch.
Soft and gentle
Like your voice.
No last words.
Nor fond farewell
Just death's,
Cold embrace.
All the while
'Neath these grey rocks,
My bones lie.
Twenty years have passed,
My baby grown,
Her now?
With children of her own
While I lie,

8,000 miles from home.

Author's Notes/Comments:
Apparently the Greeks reckon that if you still speak a dead person's name, they are not really dead. At least they're not forgotten. Like so many are.

189) One More

They'd got another one last night.
He's given up the ghost,
He'd given up the fight
They found him early this morn.
The gaunt and haunted look upon his face,
The rope lay wound around the small and twisted
form.
No bullet holes or shrapnel wounds,
No blood, no snot, no gore,
Just another casualty
Of
a long forgotten war.

Author's Notes/Comments:
Several young men in their late twenties suffering from
PTSD committed suicide prior to parades on the 11th of
November 2000. Theirs is an untold chapter in a forgotten
war, within the mind.

190) For Some of Us

We,
those of us,
left behind,
Move amidst a world,
That sees us naught.
They misinterpret,
our thoughts.
Understand,
none,
of our words.
We laugh,
we smile,
we have good fun!
But our eyes,
show the despair.
The worthlessness,
our sense
of loss.

For some,
we sit
and pray.
To help us,
through,
this,
and every other day!
The beer tastes flat.
While spirits,
both wain.
Whether it be,

the liquid kind,
or in a
spiritual vein.
Once,
we thought.
That it was
Selfish.

The years,
have changed us.
We'd oft falter,
and have new beginnings!
With each year that passed.
Harder
than the last.
Once we think,
they'd know.
There'd be an understanding...
We to choose to leave.
Not shown the hate,
for leaving.
But the pity,
For a troubled mind.
We few.
We so very few,
we band... .

of Brothers!

For only some of us mind,
but mostly... .

Class of 82
God Have Mercy on Us
Forever Young

191) Border Country

The grass looks, smells the same as home, maybe a bit greener.
The flowers look the same, the colours just as bright.
There's the same scented dusky hue that sails the night.
And when you've stopped, gone still, done your three-metre check,
The bird's song starts, branches sway, leaves rustle.
You scan 6400, the wary eye still takes in nature's beauty,
thoughts drift to home. A fire fly pulses.
And the clattering clacking of rotors fills your ears.
As the down draft, fills your face with bits of straw.
You're observing black figures in luminescent green fields.

One by one we fill the grey 'n' green machine
The door slams closed.
Thumbs-up given.
Green cockpits glow,
warmth.
Stomach churning,
the nose drops as it claws its way into the air,
while your bowels try to drop through the floor.
It's a roller-coaster ride back, but you don't know the half.
Foot weary snores, try to rise above the rotors' noise,
Black, brown 'n' green faced men, who were mere boys.

Now warriors in flight.

Author's Notes/Comments:
South Armagh in Northern Ireland is a place that has very
lovely countryside.
I've walked a fair bit of it.

192) Me and the MFC

Sitting on the side of hill
Just watching the last light of day,
We're sharing a tactical smoke
While keeping the enemy at bay.

20 B&H and an army doss bag
Head down, duck down
Lungs full of smoke
Mouth full of feathers.

Sitting overlooking the guns
Having just been dropped off
At Goat Ridge
Tactical doss bag fag

Wasn't really much fun!
Dooby dooby dooby dooby!
Apologies to a great song!
No apologies for the fag

Me and Dave (Charlie) Brown MFC
June 1982 prior to Wireless Ridge

193) Do You Remember When?

Before them,
as far as the eye could see.
Autumn fields of gold!
Although only late in May,
It was in fact their winter.
The howling freezing wind,
lay testament to that.

All saw the southern cross at night
And wondered at,
the closeness of the stars.
The barrenness of the landscape,
Of why they'd come so far.
The lack of shrubs and trees,
and why they were at war.

But what many never saw,
Were those lights in Stanley.
For along that long bloody trek,
We lost more than a few brave men.
Warriors all, true brothers, friends.
Casualties of an unnecessary war,
In The Falkland Islands...

... way back when.

194) Class of 82...

When you hear the night wind
Howl,
And the rain is lashing
Down.
Remember those poor lost
Souls.
Who are sleeping rough...
unwanted.
Through no fault of their
Own.
Forgotten by society, ignored by the
System!

School Reunion?

195) How Was Your Day Dear?

Death filled the air...
Covered the land.
It's beating wings,
The staccato of hoof beats,
As the apocalypse charged!
Lead swept the horizon.
Filled the skies.
The screams of the shells,
Joined the screams of the dying.

Carnage, chaos, confusion.

196) Life's A Beach!

The water was cold.
Its Southern bite
Took my breath!
But I did not
Falter.
Nor did my brothers!
We pushed ashore.
Waiting for the
Signal.
Which never
Came.
So we swept over the land,
And made it ours.

21st May 1982.

197) Not By Choice Alone...

Why not me?
On that fateful day,
I stood beside you!
How didst fate,
Make the choice?
To take just one...
and not, the other.
Nor,
not none, or both.
And later...
as our numbers,
Dwindled.
Lead was the price...
We'd paid, to live,

To see the morrow.

198) It's Who You Can Count On

In my time I've known...
Great soldiers,
Hard men & true.
Heroes.
Amongst them have been
A few...
Womanisers, despots, liars,
Thieves & drunkards.
All good men though.
And true friends!

Everyone?

199) Paratroopers More Than...

Mere men.
Mortals...
But sent by the Gods!
Warriors...
from the Sky.

Against all odds
Whaho Mohammed
Their "Battle Cry"
Secure the day
Take the ground
Mere men...

200) The Daily Ritual

Come sweet death,
Bringer of the dawn.
Leave me tranquil
While innocents sleep
Come sweet death,
Harvester of light
Show me the path
Through the darkest of night

Come sweet death
Your warm embrace
Turns to ice at spider's touch
While the dying says it all.
Come sweet death
Our mission of life
Tainted by the smell
Of our own blood

We arrive on the wind
Earth shattering
Its juddering drums
Signal our arrival
While it's hard to contemplate
never mind motivate,
The man in the corner, the one,
with the thousand-yard stare.

Whoomp, whoomp, whoomp
Zing, Whoosh, Kaboom!!!
Says it all

Init

Extract from the diaries of "Jock Love A Soldier & A Poet: On The Home Front: Pissed Again".

201) How Green

I learned to balloon in a brick,
Bob 'n' weave, slope slide and walk backwards.
Go off at a tangent, scythe through crowds.
Those invisible, those who're not.

Squat down on your hankers.
Bum resting on heels, your weapon on your knees.
Passed down through the ages, India, the Raj.
On the corners; still the maimed and blind.
But not beggars these.

No coal-black eyes, from tanned under turbaned
faces.
The dun-coloured khakis, now mottled greens, blacks,
and browns.
You've still got your muckers, and the chogi wallah
back in camp.
It's white faces, 'n' white teeth, black hearts, 'n' black
deeds.
The dialogue's still foreign to your ears.

The troopships still transport us here, or by plane,
herc or civvies.
No white knees to give us away now, just the short
back and sides,
With the smell of soap and detergents, that makes the
dogs howl,
Grim faced, grim facts, grim places, a grim life, the
grim reaper.

Northern Ireland has managed over the years to teach young men and women various social graces.
Some of which have been totally unusable to them in their normal-day lives.

202) Men Apart...

I need to learn, guitar.
So I can play, my brother's song.
To share, the long dead words.
And the love, once had.
Such a beautiful,
soulful song... a
melodic... tune.
That resonates, within...
my heart,
and plays...
Encore.
Within, my head.
I'm humbled, and... sad.
Of, the experiences of life.
For the people I've met.
For the places, I've been,
and... the things, that I've done.
That, they've... never seen.
How fragile, is my heart.
How, strong is our bond.
Of those from long ago.
Of the dead and the maimed.
Of men from a war, now,

never... the same.
Of men apart.
Of Forgotten heroes.
Nay never Forgotten
And
Emperors all

203) I Know the Colour of My Wings, is

Unlike, my knowledge of the skies.
I'm watching Artemis.
Waxing gibbous.
And wishing, I could join him.
For, I know, of no need, to stay.
I'm looking, for... crazies.
To share, in my dream.
On a clear night, when it's full.
Heat haze, has now formed, to mist.
And clouds, have joined the earth.
We speak, of brave men's deeds.
At the setting of the sun.
While warriors', souls, form a line
Upon, a rainbowed bridge.
Mortals, lay asleep in their beds.
While death, stalks... first light.
And the moon, has changed its colour.
Silver to gold... And now,
to

Blue...

204) I'm Weary

A long, long time, weary... and,
lonely.
I'm just waiting for the dawn.
I'm drunk, yet again,
and all alone.
Lost, within the darkness.
Where, there's no one to hold me.
Where then, was all that joy,
that daylight... brought?
It's all gone now.
I've seen some bad times.
I've seen, some good ones.
I don't know which,
outweighs,
which.
But both memories
Can make me cry.
Or laugh, like... a loon.
Forget all.
All... that, I had.
I wish, for what... I can't have.
And no one, will... ever know.
Or share.
Of the vistas, that I've seen.
Nor the silence, I once heard.
That was only broken,
by their screams.
By death, and the dying
The maimed, and the long-time dead.
Being Immortalised only,

From the images, in my head.

205) We'd Done it For... Our

I'd made it, to the morning...
Thick, grey smoke...
From the burning gorse,
filled... the surrounding slopes.
While, endless... waving, yellow grass.
Rolled... along, driven... by the wind.
We shared smokes, and bullets!
We sat, filling, empty mags, and gathering, more grenades.
The sun, began to climb, and... with the light, we could see our faces!
See... who, had made it... through the night.
And we smiled... to each other.
Knowingly.
For, it wasn't over.
But today, could be... a, good day... to die!
Surrounded, by...
Your

Mates.

206) My Dad's...

When I was only six.
You shook my hand,
Looked me in the eye, and
Told me to look after my mum, and sister.
Then you marched off to war.
I missed you then...
... as I miss you now.
And as your son...
I want to once again, hold your hand.
While the six-year-old boy,
just wants a hug from his dad.
Father and son, now both men.
Both now dads.
Sometimes in life,
It's the simple things,
we oft, take for granted!
That we miss, the most.
The soft sound, of your voice.
That proud twinkle, in your eye.
The way you taught us.
Right from wrong.
The knowing look...
when, you'd caught us out.
And the way, you wagged, your finger.
There'll be a gathering when time permits.
Brethren will parade at the statue,
in Aldershot.
We'll drink in the Traff.
While you'll be at the table,
in the great hall.

Named... Valhalla.
Where they'll call out your name.
And 600 brothers!
At rainbow's end.
Will raise a toast.
To a paratrooper...
My dad... Ned's

come home.

Posted on behalf of Jim Kelly

207) I Thanked Them For... My

The sun was bright,
the shadows deep... so,
I spent sometime today,
with old friends.
And then again, with some,
I never knew.
But all brothers, by our trade.
And though I'd travelled far,
I was told, I could not stay.
So beneath a leafy bough...
I spoke with them.
Knowing, that perhaps quite soon,
I would rest there too!
But that day, was not...

Today.

208) He Ain't Heavy He's My

I have a friend...
who sometimes thinks like me.
Who suffers from a darkness,
In the cool light of day.
It's a weight upon his shoulders,
That crushes on his head.
Brings on a dark depression,
That makes him wish...
That he were dead.
Although I know his fear...
I can't cure his all.
I can only stand beside him,
Should he ask, and be his

Brother.

For my Bro Mick
Michael Bruce McIntyre

209) Siol Nan Gaidtheal...

I breathe deep...
and your musky scent,
assails my senses.
...Tentatively... I reach,
and warm flesh meets my touch.
My eyes open... as I roll.
Meeting your, baby blues...
You've been watching me, sleep.
It's a moment, worth keeping.
I touch a finger to your lips...
To hush.
Too long... I've waited this meeting,
Savouring it oft... in my dreams.
Slowly we melt together.
For my mind is full...
of sand and dust.
The scenes of war with all its sounds,
of the... screams, of buzzing rounds
Of the dying and the dead.
My heart is yours, and I'm...
Lost now... for the moment,
in the tenderness, of your caress.
Love's stolen moments...
A memory of lust... that lasts.

My seeds are sown

210) Death, Je Comprise, I Really do

As in life, impermanence
ever... teases me, while...
Senescence, rots... my brain.
Now left to wander lonely.
I'm filled, with... saudade.
For my song lies unfinished,
causing sehnsucht to leave a yearning,
I just can't

Comprehend

211) *Forever Autumn*

To never savour autumn
Or smell the burning leaves,
Sniff the scent of pollen
From flowers and the trees

To hear the children's laughter,
Of innocents at play,
See the red of a sunset
At the finish of your day.

To hold a new-born babe,
As you shelter from the rain
Experience love and tenderness,
Or the heartache and the pain

All these things and more,
Have I briefly been aware,
But to never savour autumn?
Or breathe its smoky airs.

Capt. Chris Dent
K.I.A. Darwin Hill 1982

212) Baby's Got Blue Eyes

(For PTSD Sufferers Everywhere)

He removed her fears,
and wiped away the tears,
as she cuddled and hung on to his neck.

The smile on her face,
matched the glow in his heart.
And he realised how lucky he was.

No one can say,
t'were ever a day,
where he'd paused for thought.

The thunder rolls,
the rain lashes down.
All the while the dead lie asleep in their beds.

My turn's been,
there's some sights I've seen.
Of which I'll never talk.

The breathing's shallow,
while she clutches on tight,
to her green one-eyed teddy.

He can still hear them roar,
as he closes the door,
and switches off the light.

213) When Blind Men...

Close their eyes...
to sleep.
What... colours,
do they

see?

214) Stealth and Killing, a Disease Spread

No more, no less.
With just a nod, we were off... !
The night was dark, so black...
even death, couldn't find us.
Wisps, like phantoms, moved...
Greyish figures, lost in the pre-dawn.
No shape, no shine, no... silhouette,
just shadows... wraiths, on the wind.
Behind us,
the drumming beat, of the galloping, horsemen.
Brief flashes split the night,
as their steeds' hooves,
struck mortal flesh.
The scenes enacted in slow motion.
Those struck, faired... the danse, macabre.
Their screams...
swallowed

by the night.

215) A Dream Blacker, Than Black... It

They came and got me, in the night.
While I slept,
While I was... alone.
They took me to that dark place.
Far within my mind, deep, deep, down.
Where none can hear, the silent screams.
Nor fathom as to, what kind of dream...
It

Really is.

216) On Far Off Lands...

There'll always... be.
A little part, of me.
That's been... left behind.
Whether, added... to the water.
Or buried, in the mud.
Perhaps... reverent, in the wind.
Or...
a small piece, encapsulated...
Within...
My brain.
Which will forever rest.
As long... as I remain.
A memory... of a,
Time... when,

I once was, a warrior!

217) One of the Walking

As I walk a dusty... lonely road.
I'll sing song,
of those... long dead.
A warrior's tribute.
A soldier's... lament!
For I saw their deeds,
I touched, their sand.
I say those names.
Of who still lives, within my heart.
Whose voices fill my head.
I'll tell their tales.
I'll raise a glass.
They're my brothers!
And to me...
They're, not

Dead.

218) Those that See the Sunsets

Clouds, streaked... the skies.
Fluffy... pink, at first!
And then deepened... Red.
Dark streaks... Like blood.
Drifting off to gold... And sunset.
And, I thought, of those...
Who, no longer, see... the skies.
Or, any other, colour...
Those, who... 33 years ago.
Fought for, and climbed a mountain.
And never left.
Now remain,
below blood red...
sunset skies,

On Mount Longdon.

219) *What thoughts,*

you have, tonight...
to share...
perhaps on the tomorrow?
And, were they of... now,
or of... way back, then?
Of Valkyries and Valhalla.
When thunder rolled...
and the, heavens split...
Cast asunder
by the wrath of man!
Where death's scythe... swept.
And took a toll,
And left a legion, of...
The dead

... ...unsurpassed.

220) *From the Darkness, they'd call,*

Drunk, or sober.
When... I used to try and,
go to bed,
and close my eyes...
To try, and sleep.
I'd hear, their cries...
The ones, of the dying!
And I'd smell, the unwashed... bodies,
of

the dead.

221) I Had Faith For

I dreamt, of... blue eyes.
While, watching... blue skies.
And felt, the southern wind.
Whose icy fingers, plucked... and, stole.
Men's souls...
Drained spirits, as... it swept, the land.
While, futile, were... our cries.
Love's glowing ember, lit my heart.
And colours merged as one.
And eyes became dark...
Like those islands' skies.
Fear, became grey, like...
the clouds.
But my heart was true.
And belonged...
To

My Brothers

222) When the Time has Come to

Understand, my words.
For... I have a pain.
Which is, a tiredness... of life.
It goes deep, way beyond... my soul!
My heart, is filled... with a, tundra's worth of,
Emptiness.
While loneliness, blows a chill wind...
That sucks, the tears, from my eyes.
My hollow breath, like a... genie's vapour,
fills the blackness, of the night's skies.
And I'm growing colder.
Time to move on, methinks.
And

Say goodbye.

223) Seeking a Singer for My

I'm not looking for an orchestra to play a symphony.
Just one voice, to sing my life's

song.

On a Volunteer Singer:
Swans sing before they die; 'twere no bad thing
Did certain persons die before they sing.
Samuel Taylor Coleridge (1772-1834)

224) Seems I'm Not Alone, It's All In

I've been alone...
On the field of battle.
Lost, within... the fog of war.
Alone, in the pits of hell!
But always...
Lost, within the darkness...
Of

My mind

225) Old Men and All of Them Are

Brothers...
I stand now beside them.
Though.
I only see, young... faces.
Of, fresh-faced boys.
Not, the wizened ones.
Full, of the ravages of war.
I still hear the laugh, of those long gone.
I, remember, their now... forgotten... deeds.
And tears still flow, for those, of long ago.
Of when, we young.
And I stood...
Amongst

Warriors.

226) The Things That,

Men do...
My mother used to tell me.
Son no matter, what they do.
They can't "kill you"!
But, she was wrong.
For, here...
They can!
And

They do.

227) I'll Raise a Toast To...

Fallen warriors.
And, I'll drink it...
Here... Amongst, the fallen.
For on those green and golden fields.
Once darkened... by death.
Where his coin of passage, was, a Valkyrie's kiss and spinning lead.
Where battles raged.
Where, their blood, was spilled.
Where fate... let me live.
Though, now I'm old...
They are, Forever Young.
And thus, whilst in my slumber,
I see those faces, of the dead.
I'll dream now of emperors, and those... that's gone.
Though my ever ageing eyes, only... Youthful.
Ever sees

My Brothers.

228) We Fought the Enemy

We fought the world,
for...
It seemed,
that even... nature.
Had turned, against us!
Rain, driven... by the wind... smashed us.
Like bullets, from a gun...
While the cold, in droplets, formed...
A mist so fine!
It froze... all, it touched.
And turned... to ice!
As dark clouds, blacked out... the sun.
It seemed, that hell,
had...
Frozen... over, as had.
Emotion

And our fear

229) I Have No Fears

Death, scared... me,
as child.
For,
we hadn't been formally, introduced...
as such.
But I remade, his acquaintance,
Once again... In later years!
And I wasn't...
Scared

Anymore.

230) In The Darkness Guns Roared Once

Back at home, alone, you'd weep.
While I, in foreign lands...
I, laid down my life!
So that safe at night, you'd... sleep.
Ten long years, and more.
We've fought, that chaotic war.
Against followers, of Allah, and their swarming hoards.
And now,
I'm back home, with my promise.
That no longer, will I roam!
For now, I'm needed... here!
Due to politicians' stupidity, and, the greed of lawyers.
The sons of thieves, and cowardly bombers.
The enemy...
Have stormed our shores.
And are knocking on the door.
And it's not safe... at home!
Any

More

231) Did You Hear...

What, moves a moment
To cause, a tear?
I fought demons, in the night!
Whilst, you were asleep,
Did the music, of my madness, intrude... upon your,
slumber?
Did you hear me cry, or see me weep?
Did you...
Feel

The somnolent effect?

232) For Those that Disappeared

I walked down their lonely lanes.
In the quiet of the night.
While moonbeams danced,
On glistening leaves.
While they lay earthbound...
With a rock upon their chest.

With gleaming teeth, he smiled.
And smugly he sat.
With eyes, as black as coal.
Those mirrors, doorways to his soul... Remained.
Impassive and cold.
"We are all equally guilty," says he.

But it's not an admission of "his" guilt.

From the cover of the darkness.
Men,
with murder... in their hearts,
stood and watched...
And the banshee wailed...
because, of
"one man's" deeds.

And so...
As one, they stayed within their silence.
Though their grief, was self-apparent.
'Twas fear, that brought them together.
Of the midnight knock, of the gun it brought.
Of promises of silence.
Of threats, long past of further deeds of violence.
And these...

are not forgotten.

233) *It would Mean Sharing, a Common life*

I never sleep.
For, it's too overrated.
Besides.
Come, the night... ?
While lost in the darkness... !
I'd merely,
Commune,
with the dead!
For death...
Now guards, my door.
Who, still hunts... old men?
Oh I forgot,
that'd be...
Death

wouldn't it!

234) Brothers Till We...

Meet... that desert sand.
We march, we fight, we die!
While in between times... We sing.
When you have nothing.
When you are classed, as... a
Nothing.
You only have the bond, of those other
Nothings...
Existing, in that nothingness.
Till you either, run...
or

die!

235) No Time for Heroes

Once again.
In a land, where dead men,
still stand... tall.
I'm chasing... a sunrise!
A wattle, on the breeze,
Briefly masks the smell of death.
I've lost out to romance...
So
I'm searching for felicity.
That it may change my fortune, by...
Bringing... hope.
a fresh dawn... mayhap when colour, touches... my
life, one more time.
When leaves will fill the trees, and not the ground.
When serenity fills the stars.
When...
Perhaps, I'll just read

Wittgenstein... again!

236) Just remember.

Every, sunrise

Is a dream...

Yet to happen.

237) Once again...

My feet remind me.
Of when, I was once so cold.
Of a time, I once went to war.
Of those who fell.
And, stayed down.
Never again, to rise...
Of their own accord.
Lonely... is their slumber.
Forgotten, are their deeds.
Their dreams, now... eternal.
Their bones turned... to dust.
While my soul is ever,
joined... with theirs.
My body, languishes.
It's an ache,
of which...
I don't speak.
For, it is of the heart.
And although it has no cure.
It burns the soul,
And
It burns it deep.
It's a malady, which can kill.
But only if...
You don't

Fight back

238) It's What We Do...

Trained to kill, and maim,
TAB to war.
Jump from a plane!
Pick up shit, from Britain's streets,
Put out fires, and rescue sheep!
Standing in the middle... dodging.
Bullet, bomb, and bottle.
Live like tramps, putting your life,
on the line.
Paid a pittance, fed on shit.
But you're a soldier, so you suffer it.
Fly the flag... and,
"God save the Queen".
Fighting politicians' wars, in lands...
They've never seen.
Fat thieving bastards... liars,
to a man.
But We try our best, with what we've got.
They have no morals; they have no honour.
And for their policy,
... ..we die on foreign soil,
for...

It's what we do...

239) Hello, Was it Me...

It was... Nice?
To meet ya.
Though I'm really not, too sure.
Cause, I think you tried... to...
Kill me... late, last night!
But your bullets, all went wide.
It seems, you missed...
It got a little messy, and the noise,
was just unreal.
No cinematic... soundtrack.
Though plenty of... Noise.
The screams of the dying
Were... very... very... Real.
So
I'm glad, ya didn't kill me... after all!
1982... A crazy little war.
And in that moment of madness.
Soldier
I hope you found...
What

You, were looking for?

240) My Wounds Have Scars

So...
I doubt, I'll hear
That lonely, bugle's... call!
Above the raucous sounds,
of drinking...
In Valhalla's, hallowed... hall.
I'll, smell no more, the scent,
of summer's blooms...
Or taste, love's sweet wiles.
I'm waiting... my, turn.
While watching, jackdaws...
Dancing on a roof.
While, bombs and bullets... kill.
Some words cut deeper... Leaving.
Wounds

that do not heal.

241) Great Brothers, A Great Company

I'm holding on... to dreams.
As reality, slips through my fingers!
And who could wish, a dream?
Upon a field of angels.
We are warriors...
We are... bringers of death!
Soldiers, that are borne.
Emissaries, of St Michael.
Harbourers, of destruction.
On the fields of battle, only...
At the mercy, of the Valkyries.
Our power, like our numbers seems to ever dwindle.
From 762 to a mere 556, millimetres that maim and kill.
Rate of fire,
rounds on the ground.
But our true strength lies...
In our tenacity, and our creed.
And that would be all part...
Of our training... our selection.
At

Pegasus Company

242) I'm a Soldier Class of 82

It's just how I am.
I may no longer wear the uniform
But, I'm still the same man.
My CV may say...
Former Paratrooper.
But I'll always be Airborne!
A warrior, a leader of men.
Shown... how to survive,
Trained... to kill!
Skills once learned,
Never... forgot.
Deep down
... .inside my head.
Lock 'n' load...
Me

I'm a mama's boy.

243) A Time To

There was, a rushing...
in my ears.
And a storm raged, within... my brain,
As fire, coursed... along my veins.
We just rose up and went!
Cloaked by the darkness, of the night.
Forward... onwards... dodging flecks... of fiery light.
That should they touch... brought death.
We were filled, with... ..
Evil thoughts.
Kill...
kill

Kill...

244) No Matter Where

I'd dig.
I'd seek refuge,
beneath... the soil.
And in the heavens.
Stars, were ever the roof,
of my world.
Mother Earth,
cradled me deep...
... within her arms.
While her cold tears, soaked me...
to the skin.

I saw, her breath... sway, the grass.
As man, did... his thing.
Nature watched us, as
We tried to kill each other.
Dispassionate, silent...
Save, the roaring of the wind.
Death's screams, of flying lead.
Lost amidst the maelstrom.
Praying to a god.
Who'd...
forgot that

we were there.

245) *The Ultimate Response or,*

Death ...
Has a special,
Prescient.
For men at war.
It can humble...
Most.
But it does,
kill a lot.
A, final reminder.

246) I Make No Bones, I'm ...

Not a learn'erd man.
Though I may be wise...
In other ways.
To trap a hare,
Or kill a chicken,
Makes a mushroom nettle soup!
I've played a game or two,
And held a dead man's hand.
My friends may be scattered...
Though my family is legion,
Across this globe!
For they are many...
They are Brothers...
They are...

Airborne.

247) The Haunting Melodies of

War filled...
With, long forgotten,
words.
That caused a tear, to flow.
A Slow Death, over...
A long, weekend!
I'm drinking with my brothers.
I'm filling, my body, full... of poison!
To kill the memories
That bring
Bad

Dreams...

248) The Unseen Wounds Of...

An ache, a dull throb...
They are tired.
And they often, let me know.
Broken... twisted limbs,
Lost limbs...
... all sending.
Intermittent, pulses... of sporadic,
electric... shocks, of pain...
Which... constantly, flow.
It's nothing, I can share.
For it's mine... alone,
Unwanted reminders.
Of...
A, forgotten

War.

249) The Bloody, and the Dead...

Seeping wounds and...
Shattered dreams.
Youth, at its best?
I've let the sun, blind... my heart.
I've let war, taint my soul.
Warriors die... They don't grow old.
I'm lost...
I'm lonely, for the sounds of battle.
I've been left, to wander...
To try and find, that rainbowed bridge.
Let your dirge, speak my deeds.
On my death...
Sing

Coronach... at my grave.

250) Warriors Who Didn't...

Forever, onward... they go.
You can hear them, clash,
upon the wind.
Long lost, souls, no longer mourned.
Who wander, aimlessly, searching...
For the sounds, of battle.
Those missed... by Valkyries.
Who died... forgotten...
of...
old age.
Warriors, who'd fought, and won...
For,
To sit, and sup, and sing
In the Great Hall... of Valhalla.
You have to be struck down, dead.
In battle... A warrior's death.
And
Valkyries collect you,
from...
Where you

Fall... !

251) I've A Yearning To Be

Immortal!
When there's,
Music on the wind.
It's coming from, a smoky bend,
From whither we all gather.
Far off on yonder river.
Where, Valkyries...
are taught to dance!
And, as they did.
All the while, I watched, and...
Upon, that hallowed eve.
I stood on golden sands!
I did... but I dug a grave.
And left behind... Within,
My tortured soul.
Leaving it, evermore...
Evermore,
to be

Alone.

252) Would I lay me Down to

Lest I were to hear?
Would that sound,
of marching men.
Like, a rolling thunder!
Ellipse, a bugle's call?
Do dead men's boots, echo too?
For the sound of fall of shot
Still, travels well... and, reverberates in time.
For I hear it... sometimes,
on the wind, on quiet nights... as I

sleep.

253) *Remember Me, When...*

Remember me... on summer's days, when skies are blue.
But,
Forget me not. On frosty morns... when Jack has been, touched, then gone.
Or...
When trees are swaying, and rustling leaves... begin to fall.
For I'll be there...
Forever and always... when upon an autumn's... smoky air.
I'll be that chill... in yon breath of wind... that touched your soul.
I'll be the music... in your heart, that echoes... through the day.
I'll be, that fleeting moment... that makes you smile, and you'll not know why.
So...
Remember me... when rain has filled the heavens, or while it falls and turns to snow...
Just.
Remember me... Now

I'm gone.

254) I'm Waiting For...

That last leaf, to... fall!
I'm waiting... for,
an echo,
on the wind.
While, the landscape's been daubed.
With shades, of grey...
it's also
Tinged,
with dark reds, and spots, of gold.
I'm counting magpies.
And...
I'm... chancing, my luck.
For
I've yet to see, any silver, or...
feel some joy.
I can't sing, or,
So
I've, been told.
As the melody's trapped,
within
... my heart.
So, it's nature, that plays my song.
For its beauty, far surpasses.
All
Except, perhaps

A Dalmatian pelican.

255) It's All...

When I'm dead.
I'll drift... upon the winds.
Just listening...
For my name.
You can do, a lot of things,
When you're dead.
Because, it lasts an eternity.
Being dead...
It's all

You can ever be...

256) Airborne...

I may, from, time to time,
Sit... with opaque, clouded eyes.
That, mist... has filled!
From a long, near... forgotten memory.
Of youth, when it was, at its best.
Of warriors.
Men, I call my brothers.
Whose spirit, still lives, within my heart.
For only those,
who've felt the wind...
Beneath their feet.
Have, gone to war.
Know, that unspoken bond.
That exists... Between.
Fellow

Warriors...

257) Thundering Chinook

They named it after...
A big wind.
Play me a sad song,
And I'll cry for the moment.

Cry no more for me,
I've reached Valhalla!
I'm with the lads...
In that final RV.

Left right
Left right
Halt
Forward march
Aboooyttttt turn, Halt

Life's simple
Life's not
Complicated
Life's great
Life's for living!

Where are you Daddy?
Not me, he said
It's not me.
But it was.
Who knows when it changes?

Looking less in the mirror?
While on the inside

Nobody can see the inside
So, you just can't compare
Where have you gone Daddy?

With the wind...

258) Cupid's Dead, so...

If he weren't already downed,
by an arrow.
I'd have filled him, full...
of lead.
For, love's been too cruel, to me.
I'd rather not had been afflicted.
She will always remain, that...
lover, in my dreams.
For, she is... gone.
Wine, doesn't really do it... for, me.
I hope, you... are well.
While... vodka manages...
To wipe out, my world.
If only, for a few hours.
Causing chaos, whilst...
It does it.
So

take care.

259) R.I.P. We Won't Forget You...

While swirling... mists.
Clouded, minds.
Paper, ruffled by the wind... on
Faded poppies.
As lost souls... they threaten, to fly... from plywood
crosses.
Huddled together, from the elements.
Little groups, of those... that's dead.
Crosses...
Black graphite... etched,
Simply with names.
The dates...
And perhaps a message.
From mothers, fathers,
sons 'n' daughters.
Perhaps one... from
A

Mate...

260) Herebeorg

With nights, so cold,
they froze, my very soul.
And a sky, so clear...
I could almost see, God.
The vast emptiness
Seemed to stretch, forever.
And I wondered, who, could live here.
Howling winds... tore, and pushed... and, cut through
you, like a knife.
We were, alone...
We were the emissaries.
Of, St Michael.
We were the harbingers... of death.
We'd come for.
A war...
Down South

To the end... of the world?

261) Conflict of Mortality, Where Death

In lands...
Where the wind, was so cold...
It cut through you, like a knife.
In others, there were sands so fine,
dust clouds... formed.
With every step... I took.
Once a landscape full of snow,
so vast, so white...
It echoed, the sky.
And was tinged, with blue.
I saw all the colours, from, the rainbow...
Fill, a canopy, while dressed,
in jungle greens.
And all the while...
Death

Was the only smell I knew

262) She Moved Like a Scymrian...

Speak softly my love.
As the sound, of my breaking heart
Rolls like thunder, on the wind.
There's a shimmer, on the air.
And forgotten lover's, tears
Fall, like... warm rain.
While my own, have been chilled.
If you see those flecks that float...
Caught within a sunbeam.
They are all mine,
The last remnants of my soul.
Now scattered

... on the wind

263) I Was Less Than A Teen

While the revolution, had begun.
And I was too young.
To understand...
They sang, of flowers in their hair.
And of stuff, blowing... in the wind!
Transcendental smoky airs.
Translucent... dreams.
Of
How, the colours, filled the planet.
And still,
I didn't know

Then I went to war...

264) The Clouds Rolled On

Unsurpassed

As, the swaying grass, ripples...
There's a trickle, on the wind.
And, although it hadn't lessened,
Nor stifled, its biting chill,
It brought, a silence...
And a calmness, to the land.
I'd thought, by now.
All, my tears, would have dried.
Had ceased to flow.
But as is, with nature.
Wind, and water, choose...
To why 'n' where, they want to go.
So eyes, once blurred by smoke.
Once closed in grief.
Opened... Raw and wet.
And I saw a
Vista... clear.
And

now untouched, by man's war.

265) Death

I saw...
metal, tear flesh.
I smelled...
blood, in the air.
I heard...
God speak.
I watched...
man's inhumanity.
While Death... he

stalked them all!

266) Onwards...

We're going forward...
Because
We can't go back!
There's too much, spilled... blood,
for that.
And home, is just, once... again.
Beyond, the horizon.
Over, that hill.
Round,
that next bend.
We can see, the lights...
We can taste, the air of victory.
We're going, forwards.
To meet the sun.
We're going...
Onwards

and Upwards...

267) Mud, Blood and Gristle, Under Their

Mere hollow shells, discarded husks.
Not those, I once knew,
Silent as they lay... all together all along that line,
Amidst... the crackling gorse.
Below... the morning sun.
While all around,
The smoke of war,
Clawed... at our throats.
And hid the sun!
For Death, still lurked.
Within... their,
Sombre

Shadow.

268) Played for Soldier of

Of... the crown.
The bugle call, of the dead.
A haunting, soulful, sound.
Steeped, in tradition, and heroic deeds.
Of brothers steeped, in blood.
Who lay dying, at our feet.
Now laid to rest...
Medals bared, upon his chest.
His life snuffed, like a flame.
By cowards, in the dark.
Not on some, foreign... dusty plain.
But on the paved streets, of home.
A country that he fought for.
Where he helped make it safe.
In that place.
He called,
His

England.

269) I Now Know for Me

My Valkyrie, still your wings.
Stop... for a slender moment.
Let us both, feel... your hush!
Ripe cherry lips,
with blood red nails,
which sparkle in the light!
Magnificent, majestic.
I feel I've lost my way...
Yet, once again.
Perhaps for me,

The battle's o'er.

270) It's Spring, Do You Hear Nature

My voice is lost... amongst,
the wilderness.
Where time, is a limitless fabric, of space
Love, an infinite emotion.
My thoughts are like...
smoky dreams.
My desires,
lay forgotten... 'neath the sand.
Drowned, in blood.
In a far distant land.
Wistful oriels say it all.
A song, pure liquid, that heralds, spring.
While, within my broken heart,
I merely mimic...
Their lover's

Call.

271) There Will Always Be

That musky smell...
Of putrefying flesh!
As all the colours of the rainbow,
Cast stains...
on crisp white sheets.
Pain from phantom limbs...
burned with an inner heat.
While a salty river,
washed his brow and soaked the bed.
And although it wasn't there,
He cursed his limb...
for the pain he felt!
For...

The blood he'd shed.

272) It's all History Written in

74 saw us in the jungles...
Of the east.
Malayan rivers... with their,
Bull leeches.
Which could suck...
a pint... of yer blood.
75, we saw the barren desserts, of Sudan...
Camel spiders, snakes, malaria and diphtheria.
Which spoiled... your blood.
In between times... we frolicked.
In the lush green meadows...
of South Armagh.
Where lead or Semtex,
could spill... your blood.
From 77 we travelled... round Europe,
and the world,
dancing to a Russian tune.
Which made, our blood, boil...
In 82... we took a cruise south.
Where, we buried, our brothers who'd died.
To liberate others... who
Gave, their

blood.

273) Gone With The Flow...

And in the distance,
Just below the horizon.
I see a field of poppies.
Their petals...
Like a sea of blood.
Rippling, in the wind.
And their tide...
Seems on the turn.
But, fear not for me...
For I have done my time.
And I have seen...
Wondrous things.
Which will last...
Long after that tide's,

Gone out.

274) Castle's Dark, With...

Crumbling walls.
Feathered tails, silently sway...
Where blackened crows, now hang.
T'rattle of, dead men's bones.
Eerie, whispers, still the... night.
As cold winds now blow forgotten souls.
Over blood-stained flagstones, in

empty halls.

275) Why Would You Ask...

Me
... that question... ?
What's to you, who lived, or... died?
... and how... they did!
Blood's been spilled,
my hands have touched.
What gives you the right, to feed...
from my grief?
Be enough, to say,
Men killed men, and warriors... died.
So that you could ask

that question...

276) War is Over, Our Spirits Gone...

Belgium soil
In Flanders Fields,
We dug down deep.
Where shells and bombs
Might not reach.
We lived in mud and filthy water,
Below death's bugle call...
and man's lust.
For senseless... slaughter.
Having won the day, there are those of us, who still
now lay.
Half a million souls interred...
In Belgium soil.
Within, which you've let us sleep

Our bones forever, safe you keep.

277) Not All Managed To...

We merged, with the night!
The darkness, was, our friend.
We swiftly travelled... forward.
Walking, in a line.
But, the night... was split by, screaming... exploding
mines... and then... silence.
Filled by the rattling, of their, guns.
Death... swept across the skies.
Turning night, to... day,
and screaming shells, and bombs...
Drowned out!
The dying, and their cries.
In the shadows, of the dark,
We drifted back in time.
For, fear... took hold.
Man's, primal, basic, instinct...
The animal... Then surfaced.
We fought, hand to hand... tooth and nail.
With super strength, the will...
to live... To win,
To

Survive.

278) Let Me Go

What have you done?
The curse of...
Rotting smelling flesh.
While bones laid bare,
In the desert sun.
I've no bullets left,
The bombs were all done...
Long time ago.
Where have my comrades gone?
I'm here all alone.
Waiting... for stand to,
The first rays of the dawn appear
As I've danced,
with the long shadows
of the night.
I cry for absolution!
I crave redemption.
Just for the fact... that Death,
Well... I laughed... for once,
He got it wrong.
When the sky turned black,
On that day... when,
he filled his quota.
While the earth erupted...
Time stood still.
I was not on his manifest

This time.

279) And How Could I...

There was a stillness, to the air.
Where the weight, of the heavens...
Seemed heavy, on my shoulders!
Where without... warning,
the silence, was split...
The earth moved; the wagon rocked.
Bombs were raining... all around!
And then, they were gone... !
2... 5... or 7?
But, how... could,
I

Not know?

280) We Are All Born... Of

Nidus are we not?
We scream, and cry.
To flee, the nest.
Sprout. our wings.
And fly...
And, when we age,
Once again, we seek, that...
Comfort!
That lost safety,
Of

The nest...

281) I Heard the Screams...

I saw,
the chaos and the carnage.
Felt the ground erupt...
... beneath my feet!
Watched... brave men fall,
never rise again.
While others, keeled...
and dropped.
Full of mortal pain, and lead.
The shells fell...
and the rounds flew!
Until all around they lay,
Now undisturbed.
My friends, warriors, legion,

Of the dead.

282) Well, I've Met Death At His Invitation, Ever

At the ready, I...
Even helped, to share his pain.
And...
I've seen places, that, I don't want... to see again.
Oft I see, a row of ghosts, waiting... in a line.
Though the child in me, knows no fear.
For am I not, although alone... still, here... ?
While others, all round about me,
Have all... long gone.
And yet, I still remain?
Though
I have a tiredness, within my soul,
that mere sleep, can't cure.
For you see...
I speak with those,
you cannot see, but I, oft hear.
On dark nights...
As they scream out... in pain.
I miss, what I can't have.
And I miss it, each...
And every, single... day.
There was a sweetness... in her, taste...
That I savoured.
That I thought, that... I might ever know.
As once bitten, it didst linger.
The juice, from thon, forbidden fruit.
While, I never met, Undine.
I often wonder, of my own soul, of... whether, it'd

been stolen.
Or whether.
I ever,
even

... had one?

283) Will You Share With ...

If I asked...
Would you still love me?
If I shared with you, my dead?
The cannon's roar...
The shell fire... in my head?
Would you rejoice...
or find a voice to sing,
as the dying scream, I hear,
within my dreams?
And fill... my head.
Would you still be there
in the morrow,
while the dawn brings terror and relief?
Same day... next night.
On the re-run...
Would you still,
Love

Me?

284) Cry Havoc and Let Slip...

Where visibility,
is... lost or hampered.
It's what they call...
Battlefield Obscuration.
Wherein shit truly flies!
Bullets bombs 'n' shells.
Masked, by smoke and screams,
Rings death's knell...
And all the while,
It leaves us blind...
as brave men die.

The fog of war?

285) All Or

A neurone popped.
An endorphin soared!
And music, filled his head.
While... bullets flew,
Shells, shrieked.
Men screamed ...
and battle roared.
All the while, he was abed.
And when he awoke,
He remembered...

Nothing.

286) I Saw It... In The Sky...

Death... led the way!
And the night,
swept... across the landscape.
While, we followed, in its wake.
All too soon, the night was split.
By the screams, of the dead,
and dying.
Murderous tracer... swathed, the land, in deadly, light
shows.
While the heavens, erupted...
carving out, new features... from, the barren slopes.
Luminescent... grass.
Glowed... in the moonlight.
While, men died...
below,

That Southern Cross.

287) Morphological... Or All In...

Dead air...
I used to hide, within the night.
When the darkness, was my friend.
Spilling warm tears, on frozen cheeks.
Sitting within a...
Silent misery, that ruled, my life.
For...
When dreams, have turned, to dust.
And the winds and rain, have cleansed, nature's canvas.
What is there... ?
I was left with a loneliness...
I shared... only with the moon.
And the forgotten music, that the voices sang.
Inside

My head...

288) My Words, Don't... Always,

Stay in my head...
It's like, once they're written,
And, committed... to paper.
Laid, to rest... so to speak.
For, All... time.
They're then buried, 'neath... The pages,
of

Rhyme.

289) Wholly Unmitigated

I'm off... to the park.
To sit in the dark.
And, howl... at the moon!
For, it's the dead,
that, keeps... me here.
They tell me...
Not

To do it!

290) Similar Maybe, We're Not all

Some of us, write...
For those that...
That... do not speak.
Who merely sit, stare and weep.
For our, tears... are done.
Unlike, the others.
Who have, forgotten... how, to cry.
Their tears... are yet to come!
Each new day, may not, always...
Hail, fair winds, blue skies, and... bright sunshine.
But.
It's a new day...
All

The same.

291) I Don't Do Lonely...

Winter... is my, time.
When all, are cold... and not, just me!
I'm standing, on the edge of
Life's... precipice.
And, I'm not afraid
To...
Jump

... Anymore!

292) Their Eyes

Cold!
Full, of death, and... mayhem.
Blacker... than the pits,
of Hades.
Non, forgiving...
Just

Stealers, of Christian souls...

293) Cheers, Here's to...

Dreams...
It's not always genies, full of wishes.
Once, the cork is removed, from the bottle,
Sometimes, it's demons, wot appear!
Full of fire, full of anger, preying on our fears.
Bringing, chaos... to our lives.
While my corkless bottles, merely bring me
Sadness, and lonely nights.
A wish, to sleep... forever, amongst...
A lover's arms
In

Lost & Forgotten Times.

294) Wretched, We Languish In

As emotion, can truly blind us.
For we fail to see, what others do!
And fail, to recognise, the pain.
That our own suffering, causes.
To those, around us...
And so, we all suffer, together.
Miserably
Alone... And,
In

Silence.

295) Fate and the Devil Conspire, its

In the darkness...
Where erstwhile,
lost... in the mists, that shroud, memories.
My hands, once dripped... with blood.
I sought solace, within a grain.
And drank, to find oblivion!
But found no peace, in the realms, of man.
I raise a glass, to lost souls.
For once...
I was, the messenger.
Of

death.

296) A Red Letter

Is heading your way...
While.
I love,
to hear them... sing.
As they travel, on their way.
Herald'd, by the crack, and a thump.
Harbinger of omens, presage of death.
We're sending a message, your way.
We've sent you copper-coated envoys.
With words, inscribed in lead.
I'm just hoping, you 'll make...
My

Day...

297) My Voice is Lost, No Longer Will I

Know, that.
Sometimes, for some of us.
Tomorrow...
Is just, too... far away.
Who cares, of tomorrow?
Don't... let me, die alone.
Come, meet me...
and we'll drink, until I'm gone.
We'll drink, for yesterdays,
and do, all our living, today.
For, what is done, is... done!
And, we are, who... we are.
AND will be, nothing more.
So, save me, from the sunrise.
Sweet Calliope, has consumed me!
And I hear, the magpies...
As they

Sing.

298) I'll Feel No More, When...

My skin, grows tight,
and, burns.
While phantom limbs...
Sorely, ache!
With, over thirty years, of pain.
Snow's, on its way.
For the pain, gets stronger, every, single... day.
Perhaps, it'll end...
when, we're... reunited.
Once, I wrote a song.
I hope one day, you'll sing!
But only
When

I'm dead

299) Lost in Limbo at...

Some point.
I thought I heard you call me.
In that blackness, they call... the night.
'Cept... I was alone.
... Your ghostly, touch.
A scent that lingered...
That scent, was... you!
So
While in the depths.
I heard you... cry
In

Gehenna

300) Animadversion Maybe, But

I'll keep my love
for those
of you...
Of whom, I share, an... affinity.
Of those, that lie, long... dead.
But, meet me, in my dreams!
For a love, who is of flesh, and blood,
Is not, for me, it seems.
A bond, of knowingness...
is what, we share.
While objurgation's not a game I play
And I point no finger
And

no blame...

301) Who's That Knocking at the

Gates of Hell?
Bring it on, for
I've tasted kisses...
Far sweeter, than wine.
I saw eyes, that sparkled
More brightly, than any star!
I've smelled love's scent...
in the early morning air.
Memories, more tangible, than
Mere dreams!
Of sight, and sound, and touch.
A love,
that consumed... so, much.
Now lays spent.
At, death's

Door

307) Cheers, Here's to Johnny...

Don't, blame... the sky,
For your winter, blues.
Nor blame those, who're gone,
or missing, in the haze.
No objurgation of ghosts, for your woes, or,
misgivings.
Cry no further tears, of remorse
Nor ones, of... algopsychalia.
Live tomorrow... Better.
Than today.
Red or Black with ice...
Johnny

Walker...

308) My Life...

Once,
tears... were sweet,
brought... by joy.
Now they're bitter,
and they burn.
Though they flow, the same.
Elation, mixed with sorrow.
A melody, that... Unbidden plays.
Is sleep like death?
Just

Prelude... to a dream?

309) Just Waiting While...

Cold dawn, cold steel.
Go tell the Spartans...
I won't be there today, nor...
any other day.
I'll be drinking, with my brothers,
in the great hall, of... Valhalla.
I've had my share, of battles!
Where death, has had, his toll.
The Valkyries, have claimed me.
I think I'll be...
Having a good time.
Until

Ragnarök starts.

310) Trench Warfare, Now Obsolete...

All

When was it when,
my ache... first, commenced?
That brief spell, of supposed respite,
that has caused pain, all from... Just
one night?
To have melded and become as one,
to have drank, that sweet taste... of, nature.
Wouldst that the memories have clouded,

313) Je ne sais pas...

Who knows...
And I guess I never will.
I don't know of this feeling.
Or, where it comes from.
How it descends to crush.
Or how, it briefly, lifts... my heart.
A sadness of euphoria, that only those, that have felt it...
Know.
A full-fulness, mere words... can't, describe,
or an emptiness beyond, comprehension.
At times I cry and cannot move.
At times... I can dance, like... Bruce Lee.
The winter's winds, they oft bit me, deep.
Freezing my bones, right through.
But, it was a brief, breath of, fresh air.
A hint of a chill, that that went...
Straight, through my soul.
The winds still find me, wherever I hide.
And the sun...
fails to bring warmth, to my being.
My spirit has flown.
All my happiness gone.
Save my memories
Which are now, fading.
I'll sit by the fire, in the great hall, of, Valhalla.
Where I'll slowly roast my bones
And I'll learn a new song to sing there.
So if you're coming...
Along

Please tell me.

314) *Mordacity, as the Innocent Lay,*

Animus...
It's no longer in my nature.
Petty things, that is.
I still know, anger, and... upset.
But,
to a much lesser, degree.
I think, being... surrounded by death,
And the dying,
Does that to you.
I hold no grudges, I bear... none, malice.
When there are those, who have paid
The ultimate price.
Mere actions, trite words 'n' deeds.
With death's preference, unknown as.
How... and whom, and when,
he chooses.
Live, and let live, I say.
It's easier, to forgive, and ignore.
And so, say... my fallen.
Brothers

Angelic, as they sleep

315) We Waited As They...

I've walked the fields of fire.
Between the mortals' world,
Along the avenues of death.
I heard the crack, and then
The thump
And as it passed me by,
I felt it's sickly breath,
Then I saw them fall.
As fairies danced...
working their majik.
Valkyries

claimed their dead!

316) There's Fire In My

Death,
weighs heavily upon me.
For once, he was my friend.
We toiled, long... together.
And as such...
He crushed, the colour
From my soul.
I love... what I can't have.
And I guess I always will.
By a dream, within my mind,
I have a poet's, roving eye,
But a killer's...
Twisted

Brain.

317) Meet Me, on Life's Corner... on

Some forgotten shore, where
My dreams...
have all fallen through.
The Sandman's... gnarled hands!
Now laying scattered,
'pon, the floor of life.
To be blown... like drifting, grains of dust...
Across swirling desert sands.
Icarus... was my wingman
St Michael my judge.
I'll dream no more.
In this life's battle.
Lest, a Valkyrie.
Take me...
In

The night.

ABOUT THE AUTHOR

Jim was born in Glasgow on 31st March 1955. He went to schools in both Canada and in Scotland. After a brief spell in the City of Glasgow Police, he joined the Army in 1973. February 1974 he volunteered for Parachute training.

Upon passing P Company and on completion of his jump training, Jim joined 'I' Parachute Battery, Bull's Troop, 7th Parachute Regiment Royal Horse Artillery. He joined the Black Knights Freefall Team as a junior member and won the Army Novice Accuracy Championship in 1977. In 1977 as part of the defence cuts the regiment lost its airborne role and was posted to Osnabruck in Germany. Jim disappeared whilst in Germany and joined the French Foreign Legion...

There he made the rank of Corporal and was an instructor in the depot of the R.I.L.E. in Castelnaudary. Unfortunately, the pay and conditions were not the greatest and Jim decided to "leave" and re-join the British Army. After getting out of France, he hitchhiked back to Osnabruck in West Germany where his unit was then stationed – walking the last 80 kilometres in a blizzard. After being tried by Court-Martial (under Section 38 of the Army Act 1955), Jim served 7 months and 11 days of his subsequent sentence (6 weeks of it in solitary) having earned 3 months and 4 days remission of sentence for good behaviour.

He returned to Aldershot and joined the Parachute contingent of 4th Field Regiment Royal Artillery. There he was part of the Pre-Parachute selection staff and in his time helped train a few officers who subsequently reached the ranks of Colonel, Brigadier and even one who made it to Major General.

Whilst not training prospective paratroopers, he was part of a small team that worked directly with the parachute infantry soldier and was attached initially to B Company of the 2nd Battalion the Parachute Regiment as a member of the Forward Observation Party (as a signaller for the officer directing artillery fire) On the run up to the cruise south in 1982, Jim was given 4 hours off to get married on the 20th of April. Two days before reaching the islands Jim was told that he couldn't go ashore as he had "signed off". Consequently, Jim had to re-enlist. After going ashore with the first wave on the 21st of May, Jim was then transferred to A Company whilst on top of Sussex Mountains in the Falkland Islands due to another member of an OP crew falling foul of the OC of the Company. Jim served on attachment to A Coy until June 1982 when the unit returned to the Battery (29 Corunna 4th Field Regiment, Royal Artillery) and 2 Para sailed home to the UK on the "Norland". The Unit flew out some weeks later as in the meantime they had been assigned to guard Argentine General Menendez and the other Argentinean prisoners on the "St Edmund" ferry.

Having bought himself out of the Army in 1991 for £200, Jim is now employed by the Ministry of Defence Guard Service at Tedworth House in Wiltshire as part of the MOD Security Team for the PRAC and H4H. Previously he was employed as Group Manager at various establishments on Salisbury Plain controlling the unarmed guarding capabilities at DSTL Porton Down and DBRNC

Winterbourne Gunner but to name two, and responsible for establishing the only "Overt" MOD PAT Dog sections in the UK.

During his time in the armed forces Jim completed 4 tours of Northern Ireland, served in the war of 82, and gained many qualifications, which unfortunately are solely militarily orientated. He has, however, gained a multitude of brothers from other mothers. Jim is single and lives in Tidworth.

When not working or in a quiet moment Jim writes the odd line of poetry, of which some has been translated from English to Spanish, Turkish, Scots Gaelic and Welch Gaelic and has been included in several compilations of poetry. He has recently completed a Mental Health First Aid At Work course and enjoys the rapport of the Veterans and Wounded Injured Soldiers who attend Tedworth House. A former Paratrooper but Forever Airborne.

Some of his medals and achievements include the GSM NI, SAM with Rosette, British Wings, American Wings, Canadian Wings, Basic Military Parachutist, Military Freefall Parachutist, Sniper, Combat Survival Instructor, ADV Op Ack (he did the role and function of the Forward Observation Officer due to being a captain short in the regiment), AFV Instructor, Advanced Signaller (RSI), Small Arms Instructor... .

We thank you for your service, Jim.
Jay Morgan Hyrons

Author's note:
Jay Morgan Hyrons is herself an accomplished author. Her latest book is on release now, entitled: *And She Danced*.

My son Callum
Tomorrow's Airborne!!!

ALSO BY JAME LOVE:

IN THE MIDST OF DARKNESS: PTSD Mere
Words Are Not enough

POETRY FROM A FRAGILE MIND

MELANCHOLY MOODS: Of times and thoughts
of love…

Made in the USA
Monee, IL
29 April 2021